FIREBALL

To Helen —
We hope you enjoy
the book!

FIREBALL

THE TRUE STORY OF A TENNESSEE PLOW
GIRL WHO SURVIVED POVERTY, ABUSE
AND ELEVEN HUSBANDS WITH WIT,
WISDOM, AND TENACITY.

HAZEL LINDSEY
AND
JULIA WALKER

Hazel Lindsey

Julia Walker

GreyWalk Books

Published by GreyWalk Books

ISBN: 978-0-692-52595-1

Typesetting services by BOOKOW.COM

In loving memory

Tilda Jane Howard Lamb
June 11, 1908 – January 3, 1984

INTRODUCTION

I first met Hazel a few years ago when looking for an old claw-foot bath tub. I had been directed to her salvage/junkyard/flea market on Highway 68 west of Sweetwater, Tennessee.

I didn't find what I was looking for among the doors, windows, cast iron stoves, bicycles, and sundry other items, but I found a kindred spirit in this wiry, leathery, eighty-something-year-old woman who appreciated the creative process of re-purposing old stuff. And although we had just met, she took me into her home, a trailer that she and her grandson had gutted and remodeled to her liking.

We entered through a porch piled high with chairs, T.V. sets, and various other salvaged items and entered a room with a wrought iron bed neatly made up with a colorful hand-stitched patchwork quilt. At the end of the bed stood a vintage Victrola. She opened the top and turned the hand crank on the side to demonstrate that it was in perfect working condition. The next room, the living room, was stuffed with sofas, chairs, tables, a long wooden bench, and another Victrola. Hanging from the arched ceiling was a row of decorative lanterns and chandeliers, each one different from the others. This room was separated from the kitchen with wire boxes stacked from floor to ceiling. She explained that these dividers were rabbit cages. In the kitchen she showed me a corner cabinet with a door made from a recycled multi-paned window. It held dishes that had belonged to her mother. Her dish towels hung on old garden rakes.

In her bathroom she pointed out the tiny urinal that came from the conductor's private toilet on a steam locomotive. The next room was another bedroom. Beside the bed was a painted white metal chest that her brother had found and recognized as the one she had used in the kitchen in her home with the first of her eleven husbands. She now kept tools in it.

What she had initially invited me in to see was her newest invention. She was in the process of making a closet in which she would hang clothing from a ladder positioned over two more ladders where she would store shoes. On this day the ladders were exposed. Later she would put up walls around them.

I could not help but notice a multitude of dolls throughout her house. She explained that she didn't have dolls when she was a child, so she enjoyed having lots of them now. On a later visit she would present two of them to my sister-in-law Joan McMillan and suggest she name them Hazel and Julia.

On this first visit, Hazel gave me her phone number and said to call if I was looking for something in particular. But I preferred making the thirty minute drive from my home in Athens to poke through the amazing variety of glass, wood, and metal, looking for "yard art" materials and inspiration. Among my purchases were metal gates, a painted blue milk can, and an old baby bed with an intricate carving on the headboard and lovely turned spindles on the sides.

Each time I visited, Hazel would tell me stories about her life. The more I heard, the better I understood why her mother had nicknamed her "Fireball." One day she asked me, "Did you know I'm a movie star?" I allowed as how I didn't know that, so she told me about how she came to be an extra in the movie *October Sky*. When she heard they were getting ready to shoot at a location in Oliver Springs, near Oak Ridge, where she was living, she had gone there hoping maybe they would make a movie about her life. They said they didn't have a writer with them, but they asked if she'd like to be in the movie.

"Folks tell me," she said, "that if I want a movie of my life, I need a book first. So I guess I'll need to find somebody to write my story, which is more interesting than most movies I've seen."

"Hazel," I said, "did you know I'm a writer?"

"Would you write my book?" she asked.

I said we could talk about it. I had worked several years as a staff writer for a publishing company, but I was retired and had no desire to write a book. As time went by, however, and I thought about her life, I knew it was an exceptional story that needed to be told. And as a friend she trusted and a southerner by birth who understood her colorful colloquial language, I decided I was uniquely qualified to write it.

"We ain't gonna tell no lies," Hazel said early on, so I promised her I would not make up any stories. But memory, being what it is, often leaves gaps in a tale that requires detail. So although the events all come from Hazel's memory, stimulated at times by recollections of others, especially her daughter Naomi Gibbs and her grandson Jason Watson, I have used my imagination to fill in details and create dialogue.

I hope Hazel's relatives and the families of her eleven husbands will find her memories minimally offensive. Not all characters in this book come across as angels. But neither does Hazel. I have been amazed by her courage and honesty in telling the details of her life. She has not held back nor sugar-coated anything she did or that was done to her. I am reminded of the words of the writer Anne Lamont:

> *You own everything that happened to you. Tell your stories. If people wanted you to write warmly about them, they should have behaved better.*

We did make the choice to change some names, including one of the husbands.

I have taken delight in introducing Hazel to my daughters and grand-daughters. We hope to inspire all younger readers to be "Fireballs," living life with passion and determination as she has done. And it's our desire that older people who read this book will find their own memories rekindled and will, perhaps, share their stories with their younger generations. We hope you enjoy reading the book, and if you are interested in making a movie, remember that was Hazel's original intent.

Julia Walker

PART I

CHILDHOOD

Fireball, don't never get yoreself in a fix where you have to steal, and don't never do nothing so bad you have to lie about it.
—Mommy

CHAPTER 1

"You son of a bitch, what woman have you aggravated today?"

I don't know who looked more shocked, my momma or the man setting on that park bench in downtown Decatur, Tennessee.

"Fireball, do you know that man?" Mommy asked.

"No ma'am," I answered, wincing, knowing for shore I was about to get a smacking right there in front of the Meigs County courthouse where I'd insulted a grown-up man, a complete stranger who hadn't give me so much as a glance.

I weren't but 7 years old then, but I had already learnt most men wasn't good for much but to aggravate women. My momma was the best woman who ever lived, just the sweetest thing, but my daddy was about the worst. We never knowed when he was coming home, and we was all scared to death when he did. He liked to beat up our momma and us, too, if we didn't stay quiet while he done it.

I had taken to sleeping with Mommy so nights he did come home I could help her get out the back door fast.

"Mommy, wake up! Quick! Get up! I hear the truck! You gotta get up and get out the back door now!" I was glad I had good ears. The road into our hollow didn't come all the way up to our house, so if I heard the motor of his old rattletrap truck bouncing up the washed out trail I had time to get her coat and shoes and rush her out the back door before he got inside.

"What? What's that?" Mommy could be hard to wake up when she had been in the woods cutting timber all day.

I turned the wick of the kerosene lamp up so she could see. "Here's yore shoes. Put them on quick! I'll get yore coat, and you gotta go. Get down there to Lena's house just as fast as you can."

"Fireball honey," she said, tying her shoes and reaching for her ratty old coat, "you know I can't go in Lena's house. If Sam found me there there's no telling what he'd do to her."

"I know, Mommy, but hide in the bushes nearby. They'll hear you if you holler. But you won't have to if he don't find you, so hide good. And stay off of the road. If he comes looking for you he'll most probably be driving.

"Baby, what would I do without you?"

"You just get on out now, Mommy. I love you!"

I could hear my daddy banging and carrying on at the front door while I hurried her out the back. I shut the door behind her, turned the lamp back down low, and run to unbolt the front door. I held my breath, hoping he wouldn't see me in the dark as I rushed to the other room, my bare feet slapping on the cold wood floor. I heard him come stumbling in, cussing and hollering. "Tea, you good for nothing bitch. I oughta whip yore ass for not answering me. Where the hell is my supper?"

"Scooch over," I whispered to my sister Lurie as I jumped into the bed already sagging with her and a couple of the other young'uns. "Y'all stay quiet no matter what," I warned the little 'uns. I pulled the tattered sheet and worn out quilt up under my chin and tried to lay real still, although I was shivering from the cold.

"Did Mommy get out?" Lurie whispered.

"Yeah, and I heard him coming in time to get her shoes and coat, so maybe it won't be so bad as last time."

Sometimes my momma had to run out like that in just her night clothes, even when it was cold and rainy. I felt better knowing this time at least she weren't gonna freeze.

All the kids was wide awake now, scared to death, just waiting for Daddy to come in our room and ask where she was. We heard him bumping around, and, shore enough, he stumbled in hollering our names, asking if she was hiding with us.

Lurie jumped up to light a kerosene lamp and held it up so he could see all of us piled up in two beds. "See, Daddy. She ain't in here."

"Well, where the hell is she?"

"We don't know, Daddy. We was sleeping."

He glared at me and asked, "Where is she, Hazel. I bet you know."

"No, sir. Don't reckon I do."

Our momma taught us to always tell the truth, but we had decided we weren't lying if we didn't know exactly what bush she was hiding behind.

"You want me to build a fire in the stove and heat you up some peas and cornbread, Daddy?" I'd do anything to take his mind off of going after Mommy.

"Naw, I ain't hungry now. I lost my appetite. I'm gonna set there in the front room and wait for her. Let's just see what she has to say for herself when she gets home."

We all relaxed a little bit when we heard him settling into the squeaky old arm chair. Soon Lurie and the little ones dozed off to sleep, but I was worried about Mommy being all alone out in the woods. What if a bear or some other wild animal come along?

I must of fallen asleep, though, cause the sound of Daddy slamming the door woke me up. I waited 'til I could hear his old truck motor turning over. Then I jumped out of bed, knowing I could run tell Mommy she could come back home now and get a little bit of sleep before we had to head out to cut firewood for the landlord. We knowed that once Daddy left he'd be gone a while. Nobody ever dared ask where he was going or when he'd be back. We just hoped it would be a long time.

Things didn't always work out that good. I remember one really bad night. I could hardly breathe as I watched silently from the edge of the bed in the dark corner of the room, not knowing if Mommy was dead or alive. I could see the rage draining from Daddy's face as he stood over her. My cousin Raymond, sitting beside me on the sagging bed, whispered, "We can't let him kill Aunt Tea."

"Be quiet," I said. "He'll kill us too."

Before I could grab his arm to hold him back, Raymond run over to where my momma lay with her head on the stone hearth, her long black hair soaked with blood.

"Get yore damn ass back on that bed, boy," my daddy said.

"Uncle Sam," said Raymond, "you can kill me if you have to, but I aint gonna let you hit Aunt Tea again. We gotta get help. We can't let her die." Raymond pulled his dingy white tee shirt over his head and folded it under Mommy's head.

My daddy just looked dazed, all the fight sucked out of him. He didn't say nothing. He just walked out the door as if it didn't matter whether she was dead or alive.

I heard her moan something about the baby as I raced, barefoot and sleeveless, out the door. "Don't let her hair catch on fire," I yelled over my shoulder. I had to get to Grandmaw Lamb's house as fast as I could go. She'd know what to do.

Later, after Grandmaw Lamb had once again, with her wise woman knowledge of herbs and potions, pulled my momma back from the brink of death, I thought how brave my cousin Raymond was. He weren't no older than me. I felt shamed I was too afraid to help her, but my momma always said to stay quiet. There was no telling what Daddy'd do to me and my brothers and sisters, who had been cowering in the next room, if we was so much as to speak a word when he was in one of his rages. I had heard him say more than once, "I'll burn this house down with you and all these damn rats in it." I knowed he was talking about us young'uns, and Mommy knowed he'd do it, too.

I swore then and there, as I always did, that when I got big enough I was gonna kill him. I had thought up a hundred ways to do it. And I knowed for shore I weren't never gonna let no man do to me or my kids what he done to our momma and us.

It weren't long after that my Uncle Hal, my Daddy's brother, give me a .38 revolver. He took me to a nearby hillside and taught me how to shoot it. We practiced on rotten stumps and rusty tin cans, always shooting toward the hill so we wouldn't hit nobody. I got the hang of it pretty quick, and when Uncle Hal was shore I'd be careful with it he told me to take it home and hide it real good. He said to only get it out if my daddy was trying to kill Mommy or one of us kids.

I kept that pistol hid under the mattress and didn't tell nobody except my sister Lurie. I made her promise she wouldn't tell Mommy or nobody else about it. She was scared and said Daddy would shoot me if he found it. But I boasted, "If he finds out I have it, it's gonna be too late to do anything about it, cause he'll be the one shot. Seeing that gun will be the last thing he ever does."

Men could get away with a lot back in the thirties and forties in the hell-hole hollers of east Tennessee where I growed up. Neighbors didn't interfere in a family's business, and the law didn't neither. So mean people, like my Daddy, could treat their families as bad as they wanted to and not go to jail. Thank goodness it's not like that today.

I did know a few good men back then, though. One was my Uncle Hal, my daddy's brother who give me that .38. He was real nice to us. He'd take us fishing at the river and play games with us. He taught me to buck dance and bought me a good pair of tap shoes. He took me to the first picture show I ever seen. It was a western. I thought I'd died and gone to heaven. He also taught me to drive a car when I was only about nine years old.

Another good 'un was Uncle Jim, my daddy's lame brother, who called me "Shorty." He lived with us for a while, and he was the one that got me all excited about people flying.

"Shorty," he'd say, "before you die, man will be flying through the air."

"How they gonna do that, Uncle Jim? I asked. "They gonna sprout wings?

"Nope, not like that."

Well, are they gonna tie themselves to a bunch of crows or buzzards?" I asked.

"Naw, it'll be machines, like cars in the sky."

Now I believed my Uncle Jim was real smart and wouldn't lie to me about something like that. He weren't one to tease, neither. But I shore did ponder on how that could be possible. I knowed about cars, but most everbody around where I lived walked, rode a mule, or traveled in a wagon. How in the world, I wondered, was people gonna fly.

News was slow to come to the scuttle-hole hollows of Meigs County. Most folks was like rats with their noses to the ground, scurrying around just trying to stay alive. We didn't have no time for worrying about what was happening in the outside world. The fact that planes had already been used in fighting a war hadn't reached our ears.

But one day I was in Decatur, and I seen it with my own eyes. An airplane flew above the town and disappeared over the trees. It was the most thrilling thing I'd ever saw. Uncle Jim had died by that time, so he didn't get to see how excited I was. The plane was made out of wood and cloth and made a lot of noise. It weren't very big, but it looked heavier than any bird I'd ever saw. I was just shore it was gonna fall. I couldn't imagine how it could get up that high and stay there. I still wonder about that today. I've seen a lot of airplanes now, but I ain't rode in one yet.

Another good man I knowed was Uncle Tom, my momma's blind brother who taught me to play the banjo when I was little. I met several of my husbands playing guitar and singing at country jubilees, so I guess he helped get me started down that road. If I hadn't knowed these good men, I probably would of thought all men was as mean as my daddy, and I might not of gotten married at all.

We also had a helper in our Grandmaw Lamb, Daddy's momma. Most folks said she was meaner than shit, but she liked my momma a lot, and she was the only one who could do anything with my daddy. It bothered her how bad he treated Mommy, so she tried to do things to cheer her up, like the time she bought her a brand new blue and gray enameled coffee pot. Mommy was real proud of it cause she didn't get new things much.

One morning Daddy asked for a cup of coffee, and she poured him a cup from the new pot. He took one sip and made a face. "Tea, that coffee tastes like piss." He walked to the back porch and poured it out on the ground. "Fix me another cup."

Mommy patiently poured another cup and added sugar just the way he liked it, but he cussed and spit and poured it out, too. He tasted the third cup and threw that one against the wall.

"Damn, woman. Can't you make a decent cup of coffee even with that precious newfangled percolator my momma give you? Where is that blasted thing?"

He got up, went over to the stove, and picked up the coffee pot. He walked out on the back porch and emptied the rest of the coffee on the ground. And then he proceeded to stomp on that coffee pot 'til it was all bent out of shape. Then he walked out in the back yard and throwed it as far as he could send it. It landed down the hill in a patch of briars.

Mommy didn't say nothing. She just dug out the old rusty tin can she used before Grandmaw give her the new pot. But she looked real sad, and I felt bad for her.

Not long after that Grandmaw Lamb come for a visit, and she seen the old tin can on the stove. "Tea," she inquired, "where is that new percolator I give you? How come you ain't using it?

"Sam throwed it down the hill into that patch of briars."

Grandmaw jumped up faster than a scalded cat. "Where is he?" she asked.

"He's setting out there on that bench by the corn crib," Mommy replied.

Grandmaw rushed out in the yard, picked up a big stick, and headed toward the corn crib. She shook that stick at my daddy. "Sam, you get yore sorry ass down that hill and don't you come back without that coffee pot. I mean it. We ain't gonna deal with that kind of malarkey."

Daddy knowed not to fool with Grandmaw Lamb, so he lit out down that hill. We could see him circling around that briar patch, trying to figure out how to get to that coffee pot without getting all scratched up. Watching him was the most fun us kids had ever had. We was too far away for him to see us dancing round and laughing. We knowed if he seen us we'd live to regret it.

He finally made his way into the briars and got that coffee pot. He come sweating and grumbling back to the house and set the bent, scratched-up pot down on the porch. But Grandmaw weren't satisfied. She raised up that stick and said, "Now, straighten it out."

"What? I can't straighten that blamed thang out, Maw. It's too squashed up."

"Well, yore the one that squashed it, and yore the one gonna make it right." Grandmaw raised her stick a little higher. "Now get to it."

Daddy pushed and pulled on that pot something fierce, but he couldn't get it straight. He got a stick and banged on it, making pieces of the blue enamel surface flake off. Ever time a blow rung out, Grandmaw'd lift her stick a little higher, and he'd push and pull some more. Us kids was still tickled, but now we was quiet, hiding behind the door. We didn't dare let on we thought it was funny seeing him so cowed by his momma. He didn't look like such a tough guy now.

I don't know how he done it, but he finally straightened that percolator to Grandmaw Lamb's satisfaction, and Mommy could use it again. Sometimes when he weren't home one of us would pick up that pot and bang on it. Another one of us would pick up a stick like Grandmaw done, and we would just die laughing.

But most of the time our Daddy didn't give us nothing to laugh about. It's a sad turn of affairs when little kids hate their father so much that they play-act like a policeman comes to their house and tells them there was a bad car wreck and their daddy died in it. And they jump around shouting, "Hallelujah." But we done that. I had lots of other fantasies, too – a mule kicking him in the head, my momma smashing his head in with a flat iron, me blasting him away with that .38. I didn't plan on letting him live to be an old man.

The first three children in our family was girls – Lena, Lura – who we called Lurie, and me, Hazel. Then our brother Lonzo come along. When he was just a little thing he got polio. It was awful. It left him cripple, and we had to carry him around on our backs. I didn't mind that; I toted him all over the place.

Our Daddy didn't believe in doctors, but Grandmaw arranged with one to get braces for Lonzo's legs. It weren't gonna cost us nothing, and Lonzo was so excited. His face just lit up when the doctor put them braces on his skinny little legs and he could stand up straight for the first time. We was all happy for him, and we hoped he'd soon learn to walk with them new braces. But Grandmaw hadn't told Daddy nothing about it, and when he come home and seen them he went crazy mad. He shoved Lonzo down on the ground real hard, jerked them braces off and smashed them against a rock 'til the metal was all bent up.

I swore once again I was gonna kill him. What kind of Daddy would do that to a pore lame boy?

Even though he was cripple, Lonzo would try to help do the jobs he could. His arms was pretty strong, so I would put him at one end of a cross-cut saw and I'd take the other and we'd saw firewood. One time a man come by where we was sawing and he said, "Put a saddle on that log and maybe you won't pull him across." I weren't shore what he meant by that, but it made me mad cause I thought he was making fun of Lonzo. But, for once, I didn't say nothing.

A little girl who lived up the road a piece had a daddy about as mean as mine. I was walking up to her house to play with her one day and I seen her coming round the corner of the corn crib. Then I seen her daddy coming round right behind her holding a big old rock up over her head.

Without thinking I went running to where they was, and I yelled at him, "What the hell you doing?"

"I'm gonna crack her head open with this rock," he said.

I don't know where I got the courage, but I answered, "If you go one more round with that rock I'm gonna beat the shit out of you."

He looked real surprised that a little old thing like me would challenge him like that, but he dropped that rock and walked away. That little girl come running to me and give me a great big hug. I guess even at nine or ten years old I didn't have no fear about standing up to somebody else's daddy.

To us older kids it seemed like Mommy was pregnant all the time. She had a baby most ever year. I think every time my daddy come home he either beat her up or got her pregnant. There was ten of us in all, not counting the ones she lost. The younger ones was Geraldine, Lester, Ruth, Ann, and the baby Jerry. But even when she was pregnant she kept working in the field and cutting timber in the woods 'til her back was all hunched over. She didn't complain, neither. My daddy was a little man and my momma was bigger than him, so I always wondered why she wouldn't stand up to him. "Why, Mommy," I said one time, "you could take yore fist and hit him so hard on the top of his head his shoe heels would flatten out."

When I got older I told her I believed I could whip him. I'd been fighting with boys all my life and I just knowed I could do it. But Mommy said no, she didn't want me to get into it with him. If I'd been her, I'd a killed him while he was asleep, but I guess she knowed she'd go to prison if she done that, and who'd look after us? So she had to be tough and not vengeful like me.

Sam holding Lena,
Tilda holding Lura

Sam Lamb

Center front row, Grandmaw Lamb holding Sam

CHAPTER 2

Since my daddy never brought home one red cent to help pay for nothing, me and Mommy had to do work for the landlord in order to pay the rent on the rundown shack we lived in. I weren't afraid of hard work, and by the time I was 12 years old, though I was skinny as a rail – didn't weigh more than 80 pounds soaking wet, I could till a hillside field, cutting new ground with two mules and a turning plow, something hard for a grownup man to do. My arms wasn't even long enough to reach the handles without really stretching, so I would hold on to the bar that ran between them. It was hard to manage mules on those rocky slopes when all I could see was their big old rumps, but I'd do anything to help my momma out. I was just glad them mules understood what I meant when I hollered "Gee" and "Haw."

Everbody said I was a real go-getter. I guess that's why my momma give me the nickname, "Fireball." She called me that so much, I think if anybody was to ask her my real name it would of took her a little while to think of it. And my Grandmaw Lamb, who was the midwife that brung me into this world, said she weren't surprised one little bit how I'd turned out. She said she almost dropped me cause I come in a kicking and fighting, the hardest baby to keep ahold of she ever seen.

My momma was sweet and gentle, but she was also strong. She worked hard to feed and clothe the family, and I helped her. My sisters would stay home to clean house and cook food on a wood-burning stove in a hot kitchen, but I wanted to be outdoors helping Mommy. I hated washing clothes in an old cast iron pot over an open flame in the yard, and I weren't real good at taking care of the babies. Lena and Lurie said

I couldn't even boil a can of water without spilling it, so they didn't even ask me to try cooking. But I did like working longside my momma in the woods and fields.

Sometimes Mommy had to be strict, keeping ten young'uns in line and all. But she was fair. I remember one time she had us lined up for a switching, and she said, "I'm not whipping you, Fireball. You been working too hard."

One of my earliest memories is when I was about 5 years old. I was give my first coin, and I'd never saw nothing like it. There weren't no running water in our house, and we didn't even have no well. But the landlord said we could come to his spring and get water whenever we wanted to. Sometimes it would be my job to take two lard buckets to the spring and bring them back full of fresh water for drinking and cooking. But I had to pass a place where some men was using dynamite to crush rock for a road they was building.

I knowed what it meant when they yelled, "Fire in the hole! Fire in the hole!" I'd run hide behind the spring house so I wouldn't get hit by them durn rocks flying everwhere when that blast went off.

One hot summer day I was making my way back home with my buckets of water when one of them men, looking all hot and sweaty, asked me would I give him a drink of water. I was real shy back then; they wasn't calling me "Fireball" yet. So I didn't say nothing. I just looked down at my feet while I held out one of the buckets to him. He took a big long drink and said, "Much obliged." Before he handed the bucket back to me, he reached in his pocket and handed me something.

It was the purtiest thing I ever seen. It was a bright, shiny coin with a picture of a woman on it. She had wings coming out of her ears. I didn't even say, "Thank you." I slipped it in my pocket, grabbed the other lard bucket from his hand, and took off running to show it to Uncle Jim. I weren't even noticing I was splashing near bout all the water out of them buckets.

"Uncle Jim. Uncle Jim!" I hollered. "I've got me a bright shiny penny! It's got a purty woman on it. A man give it to me for a drink of water."

"Let me see what you got, Shorty," said Uncle Jim. "Why, Shorty, that ain't no penny. That's a dime. You could get 10 pennies out of that."

"What, cut it up in little pieces? I ain't gonna do that!"

"Naw, Shorty. Not cut it up. You could trade it for 10 pennies."

"Ten whole pennies? I can't believe that, Uncle Jim. But I wouldn't trade it for all the ugly brown pennies in the world. I'm gonna keep it forever!"

And I did keep that dime for a long time. I'd reach in my overalls pocket and feel the smoothness of it, and sometimes I'd lay in bed just marveling at it. I didn't have no idea about the value of it for buying things. I just loved it cause it was so purty.

I don't remember if I lost that dime or later got tempted to buy something with it. Maybe I come to realize what it could buy for the family and give it to my momma. I don't know. But I'll never forget how proud I was to own something so splendid.

Mommy was good at finding wild greens and berries for us to eat. She knew which ones was safe and which ones to avoid so they wouldn't poison us. I never questioned whether it was okay to eat anything Mommy ate. I told her one time, "Mommy, I hope you don't never decide to eat cow shit, cause if you eat it, I'll eat it, too.

"Fireball," Mommy said, "hush that talk! Am I gonna have to smack you in the mouth to get you to stop cussing?"

One year in late summer we was picking blackberries longside some TVA land where they had planted corn in a field by the Tennessee River. We seen some men loading their wagons, but a lot of ears was still laying on the ground after they finished and moved on. As soon as we was certain they wasn't coming back for it, we went for some big croaker sacks, and we gathered up ever bit we could find.

"We are just like Ruth in the Bible and her momma-in-law Naomi," Mommy said. That made me real proud since my middle name was Neomi, almost exactly like the one in the Bible.

"We can take this corn to Mr. Jacobs at the grist mill, and he'll grind it into cornmeal for us," Mommy continued. "It'll make good cornbread to eat with a plate of collard greens and black eyed peas this winter."

The next year the folks working that TVA land left more corn than the year before, so we got plenty for our cornmeal, and we had enough extra to sell some to Mr. Norman Wade at his cash-and-carry store in Decatur. A woman who worked at the store told Mommy, "Miz Lamb, I heard some fellers say they seen you getting that corn. And they said they decided that any that fell to the ground they'd just leave laying there for you."

"Now weren't that real nice of them? You know, there's lots of good people in this world, and some of them are even men!" the store woman laughed. Mommy smiled, and I smiled, too.

In the fall we would gather hicker nuts in the woods and black walnuts long-side the road going north from Decatur, about five miles from where we lived. The county workers was glad we kept them walnuts picked up cause they could make a real mess. Not many folks wanted to fool with them, good as they tasted, cause hicker nuts and walnuts both was hard to crack. The walnuts was the worst. You had to wait 'til they was all the way dry before you shucked the outer shell off. Even then, yore hands and anything you touched got brown stained and it wouldn't rub off or wash out, neither.

And them walnuts was heavy, too. We loaded them up in croaker sacks and slung them over our shoulders for the long walk home. Later, when I had a car, that made it a whole lot more easier.

At night we'd sit by the fire with a flat iron between our knees and crack them nuts with a hammer. We'd throw the shells into the fire to burn. We had to be careful not to drop pieces of shell on the floor, cause if you stepped on them barefoot they hurt like the dickens. We had to be real cautious, too, not to let any of the hard shell get mixed in with the nut meats, cause somebody could break a tooth. And we had to be shore little bits of the softer outer shell didn't fall in, neither, cause it tasted real bitter. But Mr. Wade would give us a good price cause he knowed ours was always clean.

One time when me and Mommy was looking for hicker nuts in the woods, we come up on an old moonshine still that we could tell had been abandoned.

"They probably high-tailed it when the revenuers come up on them," Mommy hooted.

You could tell it had been a long time since the bootleggers had been in business there, cause a lot of leaves and branches had fallen on top of the still and the metal was all rusty. I poked around in the underbrush, and, to my surprise, I uncovered a bunch of quart jars of whiskey.

"Mommy, look!" I said, all excited. "We can sell these and make a lot of money! The seals are still tight, see?"

"Fireball," she said, "we ain't gonna deal with no liquor. Moonshine makes people crazy."

"But Mommy, we could sell it to Uncle Hal and Uncle Martin. You know they gonna buy it and drink it anyhow. If they get it from us the money goes to buy food, not to make more whiskey."

"Fireball, I don't want to know nothing about it."

"Yes, ma'am." As long as that whiskey lasted I'd take out a few jars and tell my uncle I had some good moonshine if he wanted it.

"Fireball," he'd say, "where'd you get this liquor? Did you make it?"

"Can't say, Uncle Hal. I'll get in trouble if I tell."

I sold it all, and we made good use of the money. But after that when we'd go looking for berries or hicker nuts Mommy'd say, "Now, Fireball, don't go looking for no moonshine whiskey."

I didn't never tell her that later, after I was all growed up, Grandmaw Lamb taught me to make liquor. I didn't make it nowhere near where Mommy lived out of respect for her, and I didn't drink it, neither. But I learnt there was always a market for moonshine come payday.

Now, I prayed about making it. I did. And I felt like God told me that people was gonna buy it, and at least if they got it from me it wouldn't poison them like the rot-gut some moonshiners was selling. I made a lot more money from it than I did plowing, plus it was easier work. And I turned all the profits into groceries, mostly for my family, but sometimes I'd feel sorry for the wife of the man who bought the whiskey, and I'd give her the money to buy food.

With so many mouths to feed, most of the year Mommy and me didn't get much rest, but winter time was the most worrisome. There weren't much paying work to speak of, the chickens didn't lay real good, and there weren't nothing left in the garden. It would get mighty tough sometimes. A lot depended on how much food we had been able to put up from the summer's pickings.

I worried about my brothers and sisters getting enough to eat. Sometimes I'd just take one bite out of a biscuit and give the rest of it to one of the little 'uns or to Lonzo. He was kind of meek, and it seemed like he never got as much to eat as the others. I knowed I was apt to find some greens or nuts outside that could tide me over.

As hard as Mommy worked to put food on the table for the family, there was one thing I never understood. She would take in complete strangers and let them eat our food and sleep in our bed. The depression was tough on people who weren't used to being pore. Families would travel from place to place, hoping to find someone who would give them some food to eat and a place to sleep for a few nights. These drifters seemed to always find their way back into our hollow. The word must of got out that Mommy was a soft touch.

Sometimes I'd come in from a hard day's work, my mouth watering for some flitter bread and turnip greens before falling into bed, laying cross-wise the lumpy mattress five of us shared. My heart would just sink when I seen a dadgum family of travelers waiting on the front porch. I just hoped some of the rich folks in town had fed them before they got to our house. Else I knowed Mommy was gonna let them eat first, and we'd have whatever was left over. And if they stayed the night, they'd get the bed and us young'uns would sleep on the hard floor. I know my momma was doing what she thought the Lord wanted her to do, but I swore then and there that when I growed up I weren't never gonna give to strangers before my young'uns was took care of.

Since I had to work hard, I didn't have much time for play. And there weren't a whole lot to entertain ourselves with in those days. We couldn't afford no dolls or other toys, even though we dreamed over pictures of all kinds of things in the Sears and Roebuck catalogue. I was able to win marbles off boys I played with, and we had an old rusty knife we used to play mumblety peg with. And come summertime we could go swimming in the creek or go fishing, which my momma loved to do.

I do remember one time my little sister Ruth had a set of toy dishes somebody must of give her. She stacked them up, but they was made of real light metal and didn't weigh much, and the wind blowed them over. She told Mommy I knocked them over. Mommy must have been tired and out of patience, cause I got a switching. So the next time Ruth stacked them dishes up, I knocked them over. If I was gonna get a switching for it, at least I was gonna have the fun of doing it.

Me and my sister Lurie also liked to climb trees. We was both good at it. I remember one time we was climbing up a big old hickory tree and she was ahead of me. All of a sudden she started backing down.

"Get down, Hazel!"

"How come? We ain't nowhere near the top yet."

"I said get down. Get down now!" She yelled.

I didn't know why in the world she had changed her mind about climbing that tree, but I backed down. When we got to the bottom, she shouted, "Run, Hazel! There's a big old snake up there!"

"Lord, Lurie, why didn't you say so? I'd a got down a lot faster."

"I was scared if I told you you'd run off and leave me with that mean old snake."

I'll never forget the first time I seen a radio. Me and Mommy had been clearing off a patch and plowing it up for a rich woman's vegetable garden. When we was finished, she told me to come inside and she'd give me the money we had earned. I followed her into the living room, and I seen this metal box setting on a table with a man's voice coming out of it.

When I got back outside, my eyes was probably big as mush melons. "Mommy," I said, that lady's got a box setting on a table with a man inside it! I could hear him talking!"

"Lordy, Fireball," Mommy laughed, "what you seen was a radio. That man who's voice you heard weren't inside that box. He's setting in a room in a radio station miles away from here."

"How come he sounds like he's right there in that box if he is setting somewhere else?"

"I don't know exactly how it works, Fireball. It's something about radio waves in the air."

I looked up to see if I could see them waves, and Mommy laughed again. "You can't see them, Fireball. I guess it's kind of like magic. One of them mysteries of the modern world."

Well, I was shore amazed about that and spent a lot of time looking for those waves in the sky, even though Mommy said you couldn't see them. Little did I know that one day not only would I have a little old radio I could carry around in my pocket, but I'd have a big old television set, too. I would have really been confused about a box you could see people in when I was a young'un.

Another memory I have from when I was real little was the first time I seen a black person up close. There wasn't no black families in our holler, and I hadn't been outside it much. But one time Mommy took me with her to her momma and daddy's house to help put in a garden. There was a black family that lived up on the hill behind their house, and the Negro woman, Essie, sometimes cooked for them.

We had worked pretty steady all morning, so when Granny Howard called us in to eat dinner I was happy to put down my hoe. I headed for the back porch to clean up. I slipped the gourd dipper into the water bucket and took a big drink. Then I put some water in the wash pan so me and Mommy could wash our hands and faces.

"Y'all come on in and butter yoreselves a biscuit while they are hot," called out Granny Howard.

I reached for the rag hanging nearby on a nail and wiped my hands and face dry. As I was handing the rag to Mommy, I looked through the kitchen door and seen Essie putting biscuits off the pan onto a plate. I went in and set down at the table, but when Granny passed the biscuits to me, I didn't take one. I just set there looking at my plate. Granny said to help myself, but, not looking up, I muttered, "I ain't hungry."

Essie was setting a bowl of butter beans on the table. She looked at me and said, "Lawsy mercy, chile. Is you afraid these black hands done rubbed off on them biscuits? Let's go outside and put some water in that wash pan and I'll show you it don't wash off."

Mommy reached over and put a biscuit on my plate. "It's okay, baby," she said. "You gonna like Essie's biscuits and butter beans. She's a real fine cook."

After that day, once I learnt that Essie's black didn't rub off and that she was a wonderful cook, I never did hesitate to fill my plate when I was setting down to a meal she fixed.

Pore as we was, we must have been pretty healthy. I guess we owed Grandmaw Lamb a big thank you for that. She always knowed what kind of weeds and roots to use for teas and poultices when somebody come down with the croup, hooping cough, or chicken pox.

One thing that plagued us was head lice. Mommy was always wanting to cut my hair, but I wanted it to grow down to my butt. That way I could braid it into long plaits and it would stay out of my eyes when I was hoeing a garden or slopping pigs. I can remember laying across mommy's lap and letting her take a comb and patiently strip the lice out of that long hair. No wonder she wanted to cut it. Mommy had seven girls and three boys. If all of her girls had hair as long as mine, she wouldn't of had time to do nothing but pick nits.

CHAPTER 3

I was still just a kid when I convinced Mommy we could build our own house. We had lived in some awful shaky places, crowded in like cows in a barn. We was renting a little old shack from my brother-in-law, Boyd Sneed. This hard ankle was about thirty years old when his momma died. I guess he felt like he needed a woman to take care of the house, so he married my sister Lena who weren't but fifteen. His family had a lot of property because they had the money to buy distressed land when it was cheap. We had to work in his fields to help pay the rent. I thought it would be real nice if we had our own house. And maybe if we was far enough back from the road our mean daddy wouldn't never find us ever again.

Mommy just shook her head when I suggested it. "Fireball," she said, "where do you get those ideas? You know we don't have no money nor nothing to build a house with."

"Well just look around you. There's trees everwhere."

"Lordy, Fireball, if you think we can do it, I bet we can."

I had a quick mind when it come to building something. I could see how things was put together, and I didn't give up easy. I'd heard some folks was gonna build a saw mill across the road from some land Boyd owned. Maybe they would give us the slabs that was left over when they trimmed the logs to make lumber. Those slabs would make good lap board for the outside of our house.

I convinced Mommy we should ask Boyd to sell us a little piece of land to build a house on. He ought to give us a good price since we was family and let us pay it off by working for him. I went to talk to Boyd about it, and he agreed. So when the Jennings Wilson Sawmill got going good across the road, I went over there and asked the man in charge, "What are y'all gonna do with all that scrap what's left over?"

"Baby, I'll tell you what," he replied, "if you can figure out a way to get it across the road you can have it."

I was over there all the time, underfoot like a turtle. They had to dodge not to step on me, but they let me get the left over wood slabs. In fact, they started putting them all in a pile and was glad for me to tote them across the road to use in building our house.

I knowed we had to get some good strong corner posts for the framing of the house, so we cut those in the woods. We was used to cutting timber for the lumber company, so this weren't nothing new to me and my momma. I could skinny up to the top of a tree like a squirrel, and trim off the limbs with an axe on my way down.

Unlike me, Mommy could lift one log onto one shoulder and, with my help, get another one up on the other shoulder. When I tried to lift one she laughed and said, "Fireball, you are too little to get out from under it, much less carry it."

But I would borrow Boyd's old mule, Tig, and hook him up to a log. I'd say, "Take it to the road, Tig," and he'd know what to do. Mommy didn't like dealing with mules. She would plow with them, but she left the harnessing and unharnessing to me, and I got real good at it. And me and Tig didn't have no trouble snaking them logs out to the road.

I guess the sawmill folks took a liking to us. Maybe they respected how hard we was working to build our house. They would give us pieces of lumber that they had cut wrong. We begin to suspect they was messing up on purpose just to give us better wood.

When we was ready to start building, I got the corner posts in place. We held them upright with pegs we pounded deep into the ground around them. Then we started framing it in, first boxing in a sturdy floor and ceiling. We used those wood slabs from the saw mill for the outside walls. When we was ready to start putting up the inside walls, the foreman told me he was going to throw some good wood across the road for us.

I was suspicious. "I ain't gonna steal nothing."

"Aw, Fireball," he grinned, "you are too scrawny to steal any lumber."

Sometimes if they seen a board was too long for where we needed it, they'd offer to cut it for us with their saws. We appreciated how good them sawmill workers was to us.

One day the county maintenance folks was coming down the road and a metal culvert fell off their truck bed and rolled down into the ditch. They was supposed to set it in a low place so water could run through it under the road. But I guess they decided they didn't need it, cause they didn't stop and they never did come back for it. I told mommy I thought we could use it in building our house.

"Fireball, it don't belong to us," she said. "Besides, how would we get that big old thing up out of that ditch? It's too heavy. I bet it takes three or four of them county fellas to handle it."

I asked the folks at the saw mill if they thought the county people was gonna come back for that culvert. They said they didn't think so since it had been there for a couple of weeks. But they doubted I would be able to get it out of that ditch.

"I'll come up with a plan. There's got to be a way to get it. We can't just let it lay there and rust," I said. I didn't know what I was gonna do with it if I got it out, but I figured it had to be good for something.

I was all-fired bent on getting that culvert. It weren't easy pushing it up little by little, shoving rocks under it so it wouldn't roll back down, but I weren't giving up. The sawmill workers was real tickled when they seen me finally rolling that pipe up to where we was building the house. I was plumb wore out, but I had a big grin on my red, sweaty face.

"Now what you gonna do with it, Fireball?" they hollered across the road. I just shook my head.

I finally come up with the idea of using it like a stove pipe over the stone fireplace. I put rocks around it on the outside for a chimney. When winter come and we had a roaring fire in the fireplace, that big old pipe would help hold the heat inside. I was right proud of myself for coming up with that invention.

Our new house didn't have but two rooms, and with nine of us kids still at home, it was pretty crowded. So we got an old school bus and parked it beside the house for extra sleeping space when the weather allowed. We built an outdoor toilet and got water from a creek. Later we dug a well to draw water from. It would be a few more years before we could have our house wired for electricity, but by the standards we was used to, it was real fine.

That was the first of many houses I would build. When kin folk come to visit and stayed too long for my liking, I'd build them a little shed to stay in. My brother Lester joked one time, "If Hazel lived in the White House, she'd have little shacks for pore people all around it."

* * *

As a kid I cussed like a sailor, but I knowed my momma didn't want me to. Swearing was right up there with the sins of lying and stealing in her book. "Don't never get yoreself in a fix where you have to steal, and don't never do nothing so bad you have to lie about it," she'd say. And I can honestly claim to this day I've tried to follow her rules. I've never stole nothing from nobody, and though I have had to get creative to keep from straight-out lying, I've generally been honest. But the cussing was a losing battle for me, and Mommy was always bawling me out for it.

"Fireball," she'd say, shaking her head, "whatever comes into yore head comes out yore mouth without yore mind taking part. And you walk down the street calling people names when you don't even know them."

One time, though, I caught my momma using cuss words, and I never stopped kidding her about it. Mommy loved to go fishing. It was a good way to get free food for the family, although she didn't like to eat fish herself, and she found it relaxing, too. We would dig some worms or catch some crickets and take our cane poles and walk eight or ten miles to the river. We'd climb down the bank, bait our hooks, throw out our lines, and wait for the fish to bite.

One time we was having a real good day of fishing. When we would catch one we'd put it on a line we'd tied to a river birch on the edge of the water. We gradually made our way downstream, out of sight of our fish we'd already caught, hoping to get more bites. It had been a sunny day but clouds was beginning to gather and the wind was kicking up. Mommy said we'd better make our way back to the road and head for home before a storm come up.

She told me to stay close to the bank and hold tight to the bushes. "Yore so little, Fireball, it won't take a big wind to pick you up and blow you away."

We started looking for the place where we'd left our catch, and we couldn't find it. Mommy was convinced somebody had come along and stole our fish. I didn't think so cause we hadn't heard no car or no other noise.

Mommy spotted some car tracks, and she said, "Look! See? Some son of a bitch done come along and stole our supper!"

I just about died laughing. It was almost worth it, losing them fish, to have this tale to tell on Mommy. Her calling somebody a son of a bitch! I weren't never gonna let her forget it. As long as she lived, I'd say, "Some son of a bitch done stole our fish."

And Mommy would say, "Fireball, that's enough of that!"

Mommy's hard work weren't just limited to taking care of her children and the strangers that wandered through. She also looked after her momma and daddy and two brothers that lived with them. One of these brothers was blind and the other was cripple, so they wasn't much help. They lived in the Big Springs community, about 14 miles down the road toward Cleveland. We would walk down there twice a week to get water, clean the house, wash clothes, and cook food for them.

Mommy loved to walk, and she could go fast. I had to move quick to keep up with her. One time we was about half way to Granny's house, and I was sweating and breathing real hard. I guess my face must have been red, too. Mommy stopped and said, "Fireball, you go set on that bank and rest a spell."

"I'm sorry, Mommy. I don't want to slow you down and make us late."

"Fireball, my legs is two times as long as yores. You have to work twice as hard as me, taking two steps to every one of mine. You go rest and don't worry none about it."

I thought that was real sweet of her not to make me feel bad for slowing us down.

After I rested a spell, we headed on down the road to Granny Howard's house. As soon as we set foot in the front yard, my Uncle Tom, the one that was blind, called out our names. He had spent so many years setting on that front porch listening, he could tell when somebody stepped in the yard and who they was if they had ever been there before.

"Hey, Uncle Tom." I run over and give him a big old hug.

"Howdy-do, Shorty. You better get inside and get yoreself a dipper of water. It's hotter than Hades today, and you've walked a far piece from Decatur."

I hurried inside to say hey to Granny and get that drink of water. I found the gourd dipper setting on the kitchen table and filled it with water from the galvanized water bucket. It tasted cool after our hot walk even though Granny, like us, didn't have no refrigeration.

I hoped Mommy would want to visit a little bit before we started doing chores, cause I wanted to hear one of Uncle Tom's adventures. For a blind man, he must of got around more than most. His tales was full of trials and tribulations, but my favorite was the one about how he killed three men and got away with it. Nobody would of believed a blind man could do that, and that's why he weren't in prison.

It seems Uncle Tom was visiting a lady he was keeping company with. She lived on the other side of the creek, which he had to cross on a foot log. But he had made that trip so many times he could do it blind, which he was. While he was there visiting, three of her other suitors showed up. They didn't like finding Uncle Tom there, and he heard them say they was gonna beat him up. Well, Uncle Tom knowed how to protect hisself pretty good, but three against one ain't a fair fight, even if everbody can see.

Uncle Tom always carried a pistol for protection, but he had to be in the right position to use it. Knowing this, he scooted out of that house before they could lay a hand on him and hurried toward the foot log. When he got on the other side he turned around and waited. He heard them a coming, so he listened 'til three sets of feet was on that foot log. Then he shot, one... two... three times. He heard a splash after ever shot. He hurried on home and didn't say nothing about it to nobody. Later three bodies was found in the creek, stone dead. Who shot them was a mystery that weren't never solved. Who would have ever suspected a blind man of such a thing?

Uncle Tom also claimed to be a good fighter. "They think cause I can't see they have the advantage," he explained. "I let them think that in the beginning, then I show them what I got."

He give me pointers on how to fight, as well. "Don't jump right in," he'd say. "Let them get the first lick in. Let them start off a thinking they are gonna win, then you make your move."

Man on right believed to be blind Uncle Tom, other man an unidentified relative.
Penciled notation on back says, "To Robert from your uncle Tom."

I always wondered what all Uncle Tom might have done if he could see. He was the one of my Momma's family I wanted to be like. But

I loved the others, too. It was so peaceful when I went to their house. They was religious but not fanatics. They didn't cuss nor fight like some of my daddy's people did, but they didn't preach at you neither.

My Momma had gone to church regular before she married my daddy, but he wouldn't allow it no more. She was so happy when she finally got a radio cause she could listen to preaching and gospel music when Daddy weren't at home, which was most of the time.

I weren't real sure how I felt about church people. Nary a one ever come to our house to ask if we had enough food to eat or clothes to wear. And I'm shore they seen Mommy's black and blue bruises, but they never asked if she was all right. And they didn't invite us to come to church, neither, so I guess they didn't think pore folks' souls was worth saving.

But I did believe God heard my prayers that my daddy wouldn't kill my momma. I prayed that prayer so hard, so many times. And since she didn't never die, no matter how bad he beat her, I figured God was due the credit.

And I did enjoy setting at the kitchen table with Mommy listening to the Carter family singing, "This world is not my home, I'm just a traveling through. If heaven's not my home, then, Lord, what will I do?" But my favorite was listening to the Grand Ole Opry out of Nashville on Saturday nights with singers like Kitty Wells and Ernest Tubb. And I liked Eddy Arnold, the Tennessee Plowboy, cause I felt like we had something in common, me being a plowgirl and all. And I loved listening to Mother Maybelle and the Carter Sisters singing country songs that wasn't gospel, too. When I got older and played and sang at country jubilees, sometimes folks called me June cause they said I looked like June Carter. Later, other folks said I looked and sounded like Loretta Lynn. That really tickled me.

CHAPTER 4

I learnt early on that my momma and my uncles couldn't be with me all the time, and nobody else was going to take care of me, so I'd have to do it myself. I dressed like a boy, worked like a boy, and fought like a boy. But when I was about 12 years old I had to learn about being a girl. I started growing little boobies, and my sisters teased me about it. "Hazel's getting titties. The boys are shore to start hanging around now." I didn't think it was funny.

One day I rode a mule to work in the fields with a feller I'll call Otis who we was working for. When he was helping me get down off that mule, that son of a bitch rubbed on my little boobies. I had overheard enough woman talk to know what could happen. I knowed if I didn't stop it right then and there I'd be raped. I was wearing high-top, hard-soled brogans for field work. I hauled off and kicked him between the legs as hard as I could. His eyes bugged out and he stopped breathing. I was scared to death I'd killed him. "Otis, don't you die on me, you son of a bitch," I hollered.

He was doubled over. "Fireball, … (gasp) … are you … (gasp)… trying to … (gasp)… kill me?…You're crazy! … I'm gonna tell … Tea … what you done to me."

"While you are at it, why don't you tell yore wife what you tried to do to me?"

"Yore … Momma's … gonna …"

"Say it again, you son of a bitch, and I'll keep kicking 'til you stop breathing and I have to tell them where to come find yore sorry dead ass."

He finally begun calming down and breathing regular again, and I knowed I had found the way to protect myself for life. And, sure enough, for a while after that I was safe. Otis told other men, "You don't want to mess with Fireball."

From then on, I was always prepared if I needed to defend myself. I figured it out that even though they was bigger than me, when a man got excited, he weren't real careful. He'd get me by the shoulders and push me back, but he had to use one hand to get my britches down, and then he had to fumble with his own overall buckles to get his down and get his tally whacker out. In his rush to get ready, that bastard would let down his guard and didn't see it coming when I pulled my knee up real fast and kicked with all my might. When my big old brogan shoes hit those balls it knocked him right out of the mood. Over the years, I figure I kicked about nine men, in all, including one preacher, to keep them from forcing themselves on me. And to this day, you won't see me in skimpy flats or flip-flops.

I tried to teach this protection to my older sister Lurie. I told her, "If he's got a pecker, he's a son of a bitch."

But she didn't agree. "I think kicking a man like that is cruel," she said.

"What's cruel is what that bastard is trying to do to you. He's trying to take something from you that you don't want to give. And if you get raped, ain't nobody gonna take up for you. Folks won't say nothing about him, but they'll call you pore white trash and say you was asking for it."

"But you could hurt him real bad."

"Lurie, I know you are trying to be kind hearted like Mommy, but think about what it would mean for her if we start having babies. She's already got ten mouths to feed. We can't be bringing home any more for her to take care of. If we have to fight men off, we have to do it good and make sure they know we mean business."

Another girl I knowed, who I'll call Maggie, wouldn't listen neither, and she got raped. She was helping a woman who had just had a baby. In those days a woman would stay in bed for a couple of weeks after she give birth. The well-to-do folks would hire a pore girl like us to come help out with the baby and the housework.

Maggie got paid five dollars a week and really needed that job. But the woman's husband was always trying to get her off by herself. She managed to dodge him in the house. At night she would sleep on a pallet on the floor next to the woman's bed in case she or the baby needed something. But when the woman was on her feet again and she didn't need Maggie no more, he had to drive her home on a country road. He waited 'til dark, and on the way he stopped and raped her.

"I'm scared, Hazel. I don't want to have no baby."

"Well," I said, "if we can help it, you ain't gonna have no baby. We just need to talk to my Grandmaw."

Grandmaw Lamb was a midwife, and sometimes she used herbs to help a woman keep from losing a baby. And other times she helped them have the baby faster. And sometimes she helped a pore woman who weren't very far along stop being pregnant. We couldn't talk about that outside the family, cause, although it was hard to prove, if she had got caught, she'd of gone to jail.

"No, Hazel. I don't want nobody to know about this. I couldn't look her in the eyes if she learnt what happened to me."

I agreed to keep it a secret. One reason was to keep Mommy from finding out. I never told her about Otis trying to rape me or about any of the others that tried later. If it could happen to Maggie, it could happen to one of us, and what could she have done about it? She would have felt so helpless, and it would have broke her heart to think one of her girls might have to go through something like that.

"Well, I don't know which herbs to use," I told my friend, "but if we ain't gonna ask my Grandmaw about it, I guess we're gonna have to figure it out ourselves."

So we made nasty-tasting tonics out of all kinds of roots and leaves. It's a wonder we didn't kill her with all those different teas she drank, but Maggie didn't have no baby.

"Next time that man's wife has a baby," I said to Maggie, "don't you go back up there. You just tell them yore sick and to send for me. I'll kick that S.O.B. in the balls! And I'll tell the wife what happened, too. Then she'll most likely let him have it, as well, with her just having his baby and him to carry on like that."

"But Hazel, you could kill him."

"Maggie, just think about it. If he dies, do you think somebody is gonna pull down his britches and look at his balls to see if that had something to do with it?"

Me and Maggie was both married by the time that man's wife had another baby. So we didn't have to deal with him no more.

Another neighbor girl about my age told me in secret she didn't like what some men was doing to her. I told her what to do, but she said her daddy would be mad if she kicked a man like that.

"Have you told him what they are doing to you? I asked.

"They give him money for it. And he does it, too."

"Does yore momma know?"

"Yeah, but what can she do about it?"

"She can kick that son of a bitch in the balls herself."

"She's too skeered to do that. He'd beat her real bad, maybe kill her."

"But what if you get pregnant?"

"He'd make me get shed of it."

I felt so sorry for that girl. I hoped she'd be able to leave home soon and not have to go through that torture no more. How could people be so bad, even to their own kin? Bad as my daddy was, as far as I know, he never touched a one of his daughters like that. But I did tell my sisters to remember he was short, so if he ever did try it, they was about the right height to take care of him with one swift kick.

I tried to keep Mommy from worrying about what could happen to her girls, but one time I had to protect her and me both. We had walked the 15 miles from Decatur to Athens cause we had found a buyer there who would pay us a good price for our walnut meats. We had got a late start, and by the time we had took care of our business it was getting toward sundown.

It had been a warm sunny afternoon when we left home, so we was only wearing lightweight jackets. But now, with the sun going down, we was feeling the chill. When we was about half way back to Decatur, a car going our way come along and slowed down. We kept walking, but the car come even with us, and a man we didn't know rolled down the window.

"Where you ladies headed? Can we give you a ride?"

"No, thank you," Mommy said, taking my arm and walking a little faster.

"We are headed to Decatur and we got room," he said.

Mommy's "No, thank you" was a little weaker this time as she noticed I was pulling my jacket tighter around my shoulders.

"Look at that little thang shivering in the cold. Why, her teeth are chattering. Y'all get in. Don't let her freeze to death," the man drawled.

Mommy looked at me, and I shook my head, but she said, "I reckon we should," as she reached for the door handle.

Mommy got inside first when she seen there was two more men, one in the front seat with the driver and another in the back. She didn't want to put me next to the stranger. "Howdy do," Mommy said to the other men. "Much obliged for the ride. We got a late start out and wasn't prepared for the sudden cold."

Usually Mommy was shy and didn't say much. She would let me do most of the talking, which I was good at. But this time I was quiet and she couldn't seem to stop talking. They all seemed friendly enough, but I didn't feel safe, and I started planning just what I'd do if the man in the back started something.

There was one straight road from Athens to Decatur, so when the driver turned off a side road me and Mommy both got scared.

"Where the hell you going?" I yelled. "This ain't the way to Decatur."

"I just need to make a quick stop. Don't worry yore pretty little head none."

I knowed what was about to happen, and soon as he pulled over I swung the door open and grabbed Mommy's arm to pull her out. But the man on the other side had a hold on her, and I couldn't get her loose. The driver had got out now, and he reached in to pull me out. He had me around the waist, and I was kicking and screaming. "You son of a bitch, if y'all hurt me or my momma I'll kill you!"

"We got a little wildcat here," he laughed. "Just relax, sugar. We just want to have a little fun."

He swung me around, trying to get me on the ground, but as I was falling I grabbed him around the ankles and he went down flat on his back. I recovered my balance and put my foot down hard on his balls. "If my momma ain't out of that car in two seconds, I'm gonna squash them little nuts flat."

"Y'all let that woman go!" he screamed. "Quick! She's on my balls and she's killing me! Help!"

As they come running to help their friend, I ground my foot on those balls with all my weight. I yelled for Mommy to run and I took off behind her. We made our way to the main road, but stayed inside the tree line where they couldn't see us if they come looking for us.

"Fireball," Mommy said, "if it wasn't for you, we might be dead right now."

"I just done what I had to do. But I bet those bastards will think twice before they try to rape any more women."

I weren't noticing the cold so much now, but I was exhausted and just wanted to get home. After a little while I realized we wasn't far from the house where a bootlegger lived. I figured he was used to waking up all hours of the night to sell moonshine, so even if he was already in bed, I didn't think he'd mind us waking him up to ask him could he drive us home in his car. Mommy was too tired to argue, and that good man give a wore-out woman and girl a safe ride home that night.

CHAPTER 5

Though I was a hard worker, I didn't have much book-learning. I really wanted to go to school, but my Daddy wouldn't allow it. He said girls didn't need no education to diaper babies and feed hogs, and he wouldn't let the boys go neither. Maybe he was afraid we'd tell people how mean he was. Or maybe he just didn't want no child of his'n to know more than he did. I don't know, but when I asked he always said, "No!"

My momma was educated, and she could of taught us if she weren't so busy working all the time and weren't scared of what my daddy would do if she went against him. She didn't have no books to teach us with, neither. My daddy weren't very smart, hisself. One time I heard one of his brothers, making fun of him, say, "Sam don't know good shit from wild honey."

Before my Uncle Jim died, I asked him to teach me to read.

"What you want to read, Shorty?"

"I don't know yet."

Uncle Jim laughed, "You want to read but you don't know what you want to read. Well, you gotta start with the alphabet."

"What's that, Uncle Jim?"

"The alphabet, Shorty. You know, the A-B-Cs, the letters that make words."

Before Uncle Jim got around to teaching me the alphabet, Uncle Hal said he'd teach me, and he did. Then I started learning how to write the names of people with just three letters in the spelling.

"Hal, H-A-L, Hal."

Sue, S-U-E, Sue."

And I'd copy names of things out of Mommy's big old Sears and Roebuck Catalogue. I had to stand on a chair to get it down off the shelf; it was about heavy as I was. I'd look at the pictures and figure out from the sounds of the letters which word told the name of a thing. Then I'd practice writing and saying it 'til I could write it without looking.

"Doll, D-O-L-L, doll."

"Radio, R-A-D-I-O, radio."

I still remember all these years later what a hard time I had remembering how to spell "wagon."

"Wagon, W-A-G-I-N – no, that ain't right!"

I'd have to erase and start over. I almost wore out a whole sheet of paper on that one 'til finally:

"Wagon, W-A-G-O-N, wagon."

"Mommy, Mommy, I spelled wagon."

"That's good, Fireball. You're doing real good, baby."

"Lena, Lurie, look! I spelled wagon. I got it right!"

My sisters just rolled their eyes. I wanted them to learn to read, too, but even though they was older than me, they wasn't real interested in book-learning. But I had put that Sears and Roebuck Catalogue to more use than just dreaming of things you can't have before it reached its important place in the outhouse. And I knowed I didn't want to stop with just learning a few words.

Educated people don't understand how hard it is when you don't know how to read. You see signs and know they are trying to tell you something, but you don't know what it is. And you are real embarrassed cause you know people are looking down on you. So when my momma finally divorced my daddy, even though I was almost 14 years old, I went to school for the first time.

My daddy had been shacking up with a woman. He'd did that for years, and it didn't seem like there was nothing my momma could do about it. But daddy decided he wanted to marry this other woman. He couldn't get a divorce hisself cause Mommy hadn't never done nothing that was grounds for it. There weren't no such thing as no-fault divorce in those days. But Mommy had plenty of grounds for divorcing him, and I guess she was glad to do it. We all hoped that would keep him away from our house and he couldn't beat her no more.

So with my daddy out of the picture, some things could change. I remember being so excited when Mommy told me and Lonzo we could go to school when it started the Monday after Labor Day. I hardly slept the night before, and I got up that morning earlier than everbody else. I'd already got the fire going in the cook stove and put on a kettle of water by the time Mommy got up.

I filled a wash pan with cold water and added a little bit of warm water from the kettle when it got heated up. I scrubbed my face with a wash rag and put on a clean shirt and the best of my two pairs of overalls.

I swallowed down a bowl of grits and a hot biscuit from the pan Mommy had just taken out of the oven. I didn't even take time to let the biscuit cool and poke a hole it and pour in sorghum syrup like I usually done. I brushed my teeth with a chewed-up sweet gum stick, ran a rattail comb through my hair, and wiped the dust off my brogans with an old rag.

Me and Lonzo had to leave real early to walk from our holler to the school in town. There weren't no school bus for kids out where we lived. Lonzo could walk now, but his balance weren't good, so he would fall down real easy. Me and Mommy had figured out the best way to teach him to walk was to take him out into the woods where there was lots of trees close enough together that he could lean on them and pull himself from one to the next. His legs started getting stronger, and it weren't long before he was able to stand and walk without nothing to lean on.

Lena and Lurie was married by now, so they didn't go, and Mommy didn't think the littlest ones was old enough yet. It would be a while before there was truancy laws that set the age for kids to have to go to school, else the parents would get in trouble.

By the time we got to school we was all hot and sweaty. It shore hadn't did no good to dust off my shoes before I left home, but I pulled a snot rag out of my overalls pocket, wiped the sweat off my face, and gave my brogans a good swipe before we went inside the school house.

The kids in my room was all littler than me, but not too much since I was little for my age. Some of them would say, "Baaa," teasing me cause my last name was Lamb. I didn't pay them no never mind cause I knowed they didn't mean nothing by it. They was just trying to have a little fun. Some of them wanted to know why I wore overalls like the boys done stead of dresses like the girls wore. I said I only wore dresses to church. I didn't tell them that I never went to church.

My teacher was Miz Mary Smith. She was a real sweet lady, and she taught me so much. She understood why I couldn't come to school ever day since I still had to work in the fields and woods a lot to help Mommy feed the family. She told me not to worry. "Hazel," she said, "you are gonna be a real smart person when you grow up."

I had already taught my brother Lonzo some of what I had learnt from the Sears and Roebuck Catalogue, and we both liked school a lot. But one time we got in trouble. A kid was making fun of him on the playground, and Lonzo got mad. He shoved the boy and both of them fell to the ground with Lonzo on top. He was punching the boy with his fists, really getting the best of him, when the boy's sister, who was playing hop scotch with me and the other girls, seen what was happening. She runned over, grabbed Lonzo by his hair, and was trying to pull him off her brother. I heard the hollering and had to join the fray. I grabbed the girl by her hair and was dragging her off Lonzo when Miz Mary come running out of the school house. I guess some kid had gone in to tell on us. She broke up the fight and took all four of us inside. She had the others wait in the hallway while she led me inside the classroom and closed the door.

"Hazel," she asked, "what happened out there? Tell me the truth, now."

I told her my brother was cripple and he didn't have nobody but me to defend him. I couldn't let those kids fight him and not take up for him. She listened to what I had to say. "Hazel, she said, "if I had a cripple brother and somebody was mean to him, I'd do exactly what you did. But all of you was fighting, and I have to punish you all." She opened her desk drawer and took out a paddle. "Hazel," she said, "I want you to act like this is really hurting you."

"What do you want me to do?" I asked.

"I want you to holler real loud," she said.

I did my part, and nobody would have believed me if I told them that she barely touched me with that paddle. But it's the truth.

I only got but that one year of schooling, but I finished the primer and the first grade reader. I was real proud of myself, and my momma and Miz Mary was proud of me, too. Though I was married by the time school started the next year, I kept learning on my own. Today I can read and write most everthing I need to, thanks to my Uncle Hal, Miz Mary Smith, and my own determination. And I can tell you I have held my own with doctors, lawyers, and other people with lots more education than me.

Hazel, first grade, age 14, 1945-1946 school year

I was always ready to learn anything new. So when my Uncle Hal said he'd teach me to drive I thought I'd died and gone to heaven.

"Fireball," he said, somebody in yore family needs to learn to drive a car, and yore the only one I think will ever do it."

There wasn't no laws about how old you had to be or no driver's test to pass in those days. In fact, salesmen usually had to teach people to drive when they sold them a new car.

So Uncle Hal took me up to the top of a big old hill and showed me how to start. I could tell it weren't gonna be easy remembering what to do with my hands and feet at the same time. After he'd explained it all, and I had practiced what to do a few times setting still, Uncle Hal said I was ready.

Then he opened his door and started getting out. "Okay, Fireball," he said, "she's all yores."

"What, you ain't gonna stay in here with me?" I cried.

"Nope."

"Uncle Hal," I said, "I'm really scared. But I'll kill myself, or I'll learn to drive this dang thing."

Uncle Hal laughed. "I'm just kidding you, Fireball. I wouldn't let you go down that hill by yoreself."

I run off the road a few times, but I never landed us in no ditch, and I didn't kill myself in the process, neither. When I finally got the hang of it, I just loved driving, and I swore, one way or the other, I was gonna get me a car of my own. Uncle Hal found an old Model T Ford convertible he said he could get me for three dollars. I didn't have no three dollars, but I asked if he would let me pay it off two bits at a time. He agreed, and every time I got a little extra, I'd pay him that twenty-five cents, or sometimes just a nickel or a dime. Looking back, I think Uncle Hal must have paid more than three dollars to get me that car. But he let me have the pride of feeling like I had earned it myself.

My new car didn't have no doors or windows, but I didn't care. I was so thrilled with it. I wanted to teach Lurie to drive so she could see how much fun it was. She said she weren't interested in driving. Her husband didn't have no car. She said if he got one, she'd just let him do the driving. I asked Lena didn't she want to learn, and at first she said no, it would be too hard. But I kept pestering her. "It's as easy as pushing a wheelbarrow," I fibbed.

Finally Lena give in and said, "All right, Hazel. If it's as easy and as much fun as you say, I guess I'll give it a try."

So I set about explaining what to do – how to hold in the clutch and brakes while you pushed the button to start it, and then you had to shift it into first gear, giving it a little gas while slowly letting off of the clutch. This was a skill that took a lot of practice. Lena would let off too fast, the Model T would jerk, and the motor would go dead.

"I can't do this, Hazel. Driving a car is too hard. I ain't never gonna get it right," she complained. "It ain't like pushing no wheelbarrow, neither."

"Naw, Lena, we ain't gonna give up. You can do it. You just have to put yore mind to it and keep a trying."

I didn't let her quit, and shore enough, she finally got the hang of it. We was sticking to the road at our end of the holler while she was learning, but now I told Lena she was ready to go down the road a piece. She could drive a little faster and really get a thrill out of it.

We started down the road that passed her house, going faster than before, our hair flying in the wind. I could tell she was happy, and I was proud of myself for teaching her. When we got to a field where Boyd was plowing, she blowed the horn, throwed up her hands, and yelled, "Look, Boyd! I'm driving!"

I grabbed the steering wheel. "Watch out, Lena! You ain't gonna be driving long. You'll have us in a ditch if you don't keep yore hands on the steering wheel." But she was grinning from ear to ear, so I couldn't be mad at her, even though she might of killed us both dead.

I also tried to get my momma to drive, but she never did. She liked it, though, that I could now drive her to Granny Howard's house and we didn't have to walk so far no more. And later I traded that car in on one that I could hitch a trailer to so we could haul logs out of the woods. It was a lot faster than hooking up a mule and snaking them logs out to the road.

I always wanted to learn to dance. When I was about 14 years old Uncle Hal took me to a country jubilee outside Athens. He taught me to buck dance, and I had the most fun I'd ever had in my life. Uncle Hal bought me a good pair of tap shoes, and I was in heaven, dancing every chance I got.

My momma didn't really approve of dancing, but the country jubilees was for families. They didn't allow no beer drinking or cussing like in a honky tonk, so it seemed like pretty clean-cut fun to me. Once the music started, I did too, and I really didn't want to stop. And pretty soon I was playing guitar and singing at jubilees, too. The boys was beginning to notice me, and I noticed them right back. One of them said he'd like to take me out, but he was kind of scared, what with me having that reputation for being a mean kicker.

The boy who really got my attention was my cousin Hut. We had played together as kids, but I hadn't saw him in a long time. One day I was outside digging a pit for an outhouse when he come down the road. He said all he seen was the top of my head and dirt flying out of that hole.

"Hey, toilet woman, why ain't one of yore brothers digging that pit?" he asked.

I come back at him, "If you don't think I'm doing a good enough job, why don't you take this shovel and show me how to do it better?"

He hung around for a while, joking and kidding, and the next thing I knowed he was asking me to go out with him. I said I reckon that would be all right.

Now that my momma and daddy was divorced, we hoped we'd never see him again. But even though he had got married again, he had to come by one more time to bother my momma. This time I was ready.

When we seen his old truck come bouncing up the washed out trail, Mommy looked real scared. "Fireball, I gotta get out of here," she said.

"You don't have to run no more, Mommy. I'll take care of him."

I met him halfway between his car and the doorsteps.

"Where's yore momma at?" he asked

"You sawed-off son of a bitch, you bother my momma one more time and I'll kick the shit out of you."

"Aw, you ain't gonna do nothing. Yore too stupid."

"I ain't stupid enough to beat up on a woman and a bunch of kids."

"You better tell me where she's at."

"I ain't telling you nothing!"

"You damned pumped up little ass, you think you are tough, don't you?"

"Well, you couldn't pull a greasy string out of a cat's ass. And if you take one more step toward this house I'm gonna show you exactly how tough I am." By now I was boiling like cabbage. I balled up my fists and headed in his direction.

He stopped, sneered, and turned back toward his car. He opened the door and got in, but as he drove away he called out through window, "You tell yore momma I'll be back."

I threw up my middle finger in his direction, then turned and went back in the house.

"Mommy, if he comes back here agin, you let me know. If he hurts you one more time it will be the last thing he ever does. And I swear to me and God, ain't no man never gonna do me like he done you."

"Fireball honey, you don't know what's gonna happen to you."

"Well, a man might fight me, and he might win. But I'm gonna fight back. And if he wins that round, it don't take too much to pull the trigger on a gun."

By this time my brother Lester was big enough to fight, too. People said he was mean as me; said he'd fight a circle saw and it a running. And he hated my daddy as much as I did. We made a plan about what we'd do if he come back. "You know, Hazel," Lester said, "if we go after him, we gonna have to kill him."

I knowed he was right, so we started working on a plan about what we'd do and what we'd say afterwards if we was arrested. But we never had to work that plan, cause he didn't come back again. And although I never forgave my Daddy, in time, Lester did. He even paid for his funeral when he died. I just went to his burial to be sure they put the right bastard in that box.

PART II

HUSBANDS

I ain't afraid to love a man. I ain't afraid to shoot him, neither.
—Annie Oakley

CHAPTER 6:
HERSHEL RICKER

Hershel Clay Ricker and Hazel Lamb Ricker

I said I weren't never gonna get married, but I did. My first husband was my cousin Hershel Ricker, who folks called Hut. His momma, who had died some years before, was my daddy's sister Necie. Lurie, my sister just older than me, had married his brother, Daniel.

Hut and Dan was both big old good-looking fellows with the dark hair and skin that come from the Cherokees on the Lamb side of the family. I'd knowed them boys since I was a little girl. I used to shoot marbles with them, and I usually won. To this day I've still got a big old jar of marbles I won off of them. Some of them are real pretty cat eyes. I like to look at them and remember that there was some fun times when I was little.

I was still just a kid at fifteen when I married Hut. But in those days it weren't nothing unusual for girls to get married even at twelve or thirteen, practically going from diapers to husbands. In fact, in big families, especially pore ones like mine, it was kind of expected that you'd marry and move on out early. I'd seen a lot more of life than most girls that age have today, so I guess I was ready. My momma didn't seem to mind my getting married young like she did. She went to the courthouse with us to sign the papers since I was underage. I'm shore she was hoping things would turn out better for me than they had for her. Hut was twenty years old and worked regular cutting timber, more than my daddy ever done.

And things did start out all right with me and Hut. After all, he knowed what he was getting into. Folks didn't call me Fireball for nothing. We was both of us from families with ten children, so we was familiar with hard times. At first we lived with his daddy, who was my uncle, but I called him Poppy. Poppy saw I was a hard worker, and he appreciated my help both in the house and in his fields. After his wife died in childbirth, he never did get married again.

Poppy's house weren't too far away from my momma's, so I was able to visit her when I had time. She was glad when I come cause she liked to see me, but she also said the kids was better when I was there. Mommy was pretty easy on them cause she didn't like to whip them. I didn't neither, but they didn't know that for shore, so when I told them to behave, they was scared not to.

Soon after me and Hut was married I got pregnant. That didn't slow me down none. I still worked hard and kept plowing fields even when my belly got so big I couldn't hardly hook the galluses on my overalls. When I started into labor, we sent for our Grandmaw Lamb, and she come and delivered our baby girl who we named Polly Jean.

Polly Jean was so pretty. She had a full head of dark brown hair, and she was a real sweet little thing. I liked being a momma, and I think I was a good one, too. But the happiness was cut short when she got sick with meningitis when she weren't even a year old. One morning when she woke up she didn't look right. At first I didn't think nothing about it, but she was usually happy and playful and now she didn't seem to have no spark. I kept trying to get her to nurse, but she just wouldn't take the nipple, and then she started vomiting and her arms and legs started jerking. Hut had already gone to the woods to cut cordwood, so I asked Poppy what he thought I should do. He said she didn't look good and maybe I ought to put her in my car and take her to my momma's house.

I laid my baby on a blanket beside me on the front seat of my car. I was real scared, but I couldn't go very fast cause the dirt road was rutted and bumpy, and I had to keep one hand on Polly Jean to keep her from bouncing off the seat and onto the floor.

"Please, dear God," I was praying real hard, "please let my baby be okay. Please don't let nothing bad be wrong with her."

By the time I got to Mommy's house Polly Jean was real still and her eyes had a faraway look. They was open but it didn't look like she was seeing nothing.

Mommy opened the screen door when she seen me drive up. I guess she sensed something weren't right, cause she didn't wait for me to get out of the car. "Is something the matter?" she called out.

"It's Polly Jean, Mommy. She ain't acting normal."

Mommy took one look at her and the worried look on her face deepened. That made me even scareder.

"What do you think is wrong with her, Mommy?"

"I don't know, baby, but she don't look good."

"Do you think we ought to go get Grandmaw Lamb?" I asked.

"Naw, honey, I think we better take her to Doctor Ellison in Decatur," Mommy said, taking off her apron and getting into the car.

Mommy was holding Polly Jean now, so I could go faster. I was still praying real hard that God wouldn't let nothing terrible be wrong with my baby.

When we got to the doctor's office there was people in the waiting room, but I rushed right past them to where I seen the doctor. "You've got to help my baby, doctor," I begged. "She's real bad."

The doctor said to lay her on the table and he'd look at her. He lifted her arms and legs, and then he tried to turn her head to one side and then the other, but he couldn't move it.

"What's wrong with her?" I asked.

Dr. Ellison took a deep breath and shook his head. "Meningitis." he said. "There's nothing I can do for this baby. She'll be dead in fifteen minutes." He walked out of the room.

I stood there dazed, alone, and confused. I picked Polly Jean up and held her real close to my breast. "Let's go home, baby," I whispered, not taking in what I had just heard. Mommy followed me out the door and held Polly Jean as we drove home, not asking nothing. I think she already knowed what the doctor was gonna say. We prayed as hard as we could, but there weren't nothing gonna save her now. My eyes was burning as I grasped the steering wheel, but there wasn't no tears yet. By the time we got home, she was gone.

I don't remember very much what happened the rest of that day and the next. Hut was beside me, looking so sad, his eyes red from crying, when we went to see Polly Jean in her little pine box. Grandmaw Lamb, who had prepared many a baby for burial, had put her in a pretty pink dress. She looked like a doll. We buried her at the Walnut Grove Cemetery between Decatur and Athens. It was the saddest day of my life.

I got back to working out of doors as much as possible so I would be real tired at night when missing Polly Jean was the hardest. Staying busy also kept me from dwelling too much on that doctor, who, now that I could think on it, must have been a heartless bastard to walk out leaving a scared young girl and her dying baby like that. He could of at least called my momma to come back there to comfort me. I was also sad for other families that I heard about where meningitis struck. Some of them felt so guilty cause they didn't even take their young'uns to the doctor.

I wanted to tell them all not to blame theirselves. Taking Polly Jean to that doctor hadn't done her no good.

For a while I didn't think I wanted to have no more babies. I didn't understand why I had to lose Polly Jean, and I shore didn't want to have to suffer like that no more. But it weren't long before I got pregnant again. We hoped maybe a new baby would ease our sadness some.

With me working so hard I was able to get enough money together to put a down payment on a piece of land. I bought an old used trailer, and Hut and me moved into it. After a while Lurie and Dan asked if they could move in with us. I weren't real crazy about the idea, but I said okay. Dan was running around on my sister, and she knowed it, too. I told Lurie she ought to leave that son of a bitch, but she just kept forgiving him.

"I love him," she'd sob every time she caught him with another woman. "And I know he loves me and these young'uns. He just has to get that wildness out of his system."

"Yeah, like our daddy did, huh?" I was pure disgusted.

Hut and Dan liked to drink moonshine, but I didn't allow no drinking in my house. They also liked to play cards. One night they went out together in my car, a little blue convertible that I had bought and paid for myself. We thought they was playing cards, but later, when me and Lurie was getting ready for bed, we heard a car come speeding up Ricker Hollow. We looked out and it was the two of them with some trashy women they had picked up. They was drunk and hollering about how much fun these "ladies" was. They said they was grown up men and could do whatever they pleased, and we couldn't stop them.

Lurie started crying. She ran outside and was hollering for Dan to come back home. I was just mad. I got my rifle and shot over their heads. I didn't want to hit my car and mess it up, but I wanted to scare them good. I dragged Lurie back in the house and bolted the door.

"They ain't sleeping in here tonight," I said to Lurie. "They can sleep with those whores or they can sleep on the ground. I don't care if it's colder than a well digger's ass, they ain't getting back in here."

"But, Hazel," Lurie sniveled, "they'll get mad at us. I don't want Dan to leave me. You know I need him."

"What you need is to get yoreself a backbone, girl. It ain't gonna get no better if you don't put yore foot down about his drinking and running around. Are you gonna put up with what Mommy did with our rotten-ass daddy? Well, not me, sister."

"What you gonna do about it, Hazel? What other choice you got?"

"I can shoot his ass off. That's what I can do," I replied.

Lurie cried half the night, keeping me awake. Hut and Dan come back some time in the wee hours begging us to open the door and let them in.

"I swear, Hazel, I was drunk," Hut whined. "I didn't know what I was doing. Nothing happened with me and that old gal. I don't even know her name."

"Well," I said, "you just sleep it off under that oak tree, and I bet next time you will think about what you are doing."

"Hut, you ought to go in there and whip her ass," I heard Dan drunkenly mouthing off. "You make her let us in. I ain't sleeping on no hard ground."

"You try getting in there if you are brave enough. I know better," Hut replied. "You get yore hand inside that door and she's likely to cut it off with her Barlow knife. Looks like I'm gonna be sleeping in the car tonight. You got the front seat if you want it. I'm taking the back."

I wouldn't let them back in for a couple of days. Lurie wanted to take them something to eat, but I said, "You go out there you ain't getting back in neither."

I took the keys to my car back and dared Hut to take off in it again to go joy riding with some cheap woman. But later I found out he was doing just like Dan, and I weren't gonna put up with no cheating. When I raised a ruckus about it he slapped me across the face.

"You son of a bitch," I said, "if you hit me again I'll kill you. And as soon as this baby comes I'm leaving. Ain't no sorry-ass bastard gonna do me the way my daddy done my momma."

"Aw, shut up, Hazel. You and yore big mouth. You know you ain't going nowhere."

"You just watch me. And if you know which side yore bread is buttered on you'll keep yore distance 'til I've had this baby. Then I'll keep mine."

My belly got even fatter this time, so I figured I was gonna have a big baby. But I hadn't had no trouble birthing Polly Jean, so I didn't expect no problems this time neither. When I started into labor, I sent for Grandmaw Lamb like before. But we waited all day long, and nothing happened. By the second day, I was real tired, but Grandmaw Lamb said it would come when it was ready. Mommy was with me, too, and I could tell she was getting worried. By afternoon it still hadn't come, so Grandmaw Lamb said maybe she should take a look. Her examination showed the baby was headed the wrong way. It was coming feet first. She tried to turn it by pressing on my belly, but she said it was too big and there weren't enough room for it to turn around.

On the third day the pain got so bad I passed out, and my momma said they better take me to the hospital in Cleveland. The doctor there cut me open to get the baby out. When I woke up they showed me this big old young'un and said it was my baby boy. I said it couldn't be cause my baby was a pretty little girl. Mommy said, "No, honey. Your first baby was a girl, but this time you have a ten pound baby boy."

They had him in a little old pink girl dress that was way too small for him, And it looked like five of them ten pounds was around his neck. I never seen such a fat baby in my life. "That ain't my baby. They are trying to give me one that somebody else don't want," I argued.

It took a lot of Mommy's explaining and the drugs wearing off to get me to believe this really was my baby boy and I was gonna love him just as much as I had loved Polly Jean.

I named my boy, who was born on May 17, 1949, Dallas Marshall Ricker. By the time we left the hospital ten days later, I was real proud of him. But I hadn't forgiven Hut, so I took Dallas to my momma's house. He was a good baby, and I was enjoying being a momma again.

Dallas Ricker (right) with Lurie's daughter Lottie Mae. Six days difference in age.

He was a fat little booger, but I thought, with his head of dark curly hair, he was getting prettier all the time.

It weren't long before Hut showed up at my momma's house, and she let him move right in there, too. I couldn't believe she done that. I guess she was raised to believe husbands had rights, but I had seen what that done to her, and I weren't having none of it. I thought about moving back to the trailer, but I was shore Hut would just follow me there. Besides, it was filling up fast with Lurie and Dan's family. She had a baby about the same time I did and was pregnant again.

So I talked to Poppy, and he said me and the baby could come stay with him and he wouldn't let Hut bother me none. So me and Dallas settled in at his house, and we was getting along real good. Poppy was a kind man, a real gentleman, unlike Hut and Dan. I did most of the cooking, cleaning, and washing clothes, but Poppy helped me a whole bunch with the heaviest work. He would bring buckets of water up from the spring and make the fires for washing clothes.

Hut kept trying to get me to take him back, but I weren't listening to none of his bull crappy. One summer day I was cooking dinner on a hot wood-burning stove, and I had the kitchen door propped open, trying to catch a little breeze, when Hut showed up. Poppy had gone down to the spring for water. He was carrying two bucketsful when he come round the corner of the house and seen Hut had me by the arm trying to jerk me out the door. He dropped them two buckets of water.

"Boy, are you crazy? I'll roll you down that hill. You set her back where she was."

Poppy's house was on the side of a mountain, and there was paths going up through the woods.

"You see that trail, boy? You hit that hill and don't come back 'til I send for you."

"Shorty," Poppy said to me, "if he comes back, you call out for me the minute he comes in view." I knowed for shore then that me and Dallas was real safe with Poppy.

One of Hut's sisters, Bertie, and a younger brother, Otis, was still living at home. Bertie had a boyfriend, and sometimes she would walk through the woods to get to the place where she would meet up with him. One time she had borrowed a dress from a married sister, Stella, and she decided she would take it half-way to Stella's house when going to meet her boyfriend. Her plan was to hang it on a tree limb, and then pick it up on her way back, and take it to her sister's.

Otis was playing out in the woods, and he come up on the dress hanging there on that branch. He run home all excited. "Poppy! Poppy!" he cried. "Bertie's done gone and lost her mind. She took off her dress and left in the woods. She's gone to meet her boyfriend naked!"

We all had a good laugh about that when she got back home and explained herself.

After we got divorced, Hut moved to Ohio looking for work, and he got married again. I hoped he would be a better husband to his second wife, Selene, than he was to me. I thought maybe she would have more patience to teach him how to behave. But although him and Selene stayed together and had six children, I later learnt from his daughter Cathy that he was even worse to her momma than he was to me.

When Hut died, many years later, his family brought him back to Decatur to be buried. They said he wanted to be put longside Polly Jean. By this time Dallas was a grown man with a good job. So even though his daddy hadn't paid him much attention when he was growing up, he wanted to help out with the funeral expenses. That's when he met most of his half-brothers and half-sisters from Ohio.

Cathy said she believed her daddy felt bad about how he had treated them. Right before he died he told her momma he wished he had told her and the kids just how good he thought they were. And he said he didn't want to see none of them die before him. So, except for Polly Jean, I guess he got that wish.

I went to Hut's funeral. I set down on a pew toward the rear, but Cathy come back there to where I was. "Hazel," she said, "you come up front with Dallas and the rest of the family where you belong." I went. I figured it was okay to do like she said since Hut was my cousin and my boy's daddy. I would become real good friends with Cathy, and to this day she always comes to see me when she is passing this way.

CHAPTER 7:
AFTER HERSHEL, BEFORE OAKRIDGE

I kept working at all kinds of jobs including helping Mr. Watson, who owned a grocery store in Decatur. He sold fresh produce that I helped gather from his fields. I also run errands for him. Since I could drive a car, he would send me to Athens for supplies.

The folks at the saw mill where I got lumber for our first house offered me a job, but Mommy was against it. She said she didn't want me working with a bunch of men and me the only female. I respected her, so I didn't point out it was probably a lot safer than going to the fields to work with just one man. If one of them saw mill fellers had acted up, the others would most likely of taken up for me.

I decided it was time for me to build me a house on my land where I had the trailer that Lurie and Daniel was staying in. So I started looking for cheap lumber. There was a God-awful old building right in the heart of Decatur that had been vacant for a long time and was practically falling in. It was on the corner of two main roads, one leading to Athens and the other to Cleveland, right across the street from the court house. It had once held a store, a warehouse, and a boarding house. I asked Mommy if she wanted to help me tear it down if we could get the owner to let us do it in exchange for the materials.

"Lordy, Fireball, if you want to try it, we'll do it," she sighed. Mommy weren't so fast to see opportunities as me, but she was always willing to work. When I went to see the owner he said he had been wanting to get that eyesore tore down. He was happy to make a deal, and we was anxious to get started. We showed up early the next morning, hammers in hand, and begun tearing down the building. I started out on the roof. After I got the roofing material off, I loosened each plank and handed it down, board by board, to Mommy, and she loaded it onto the old pickup truck I had traded my car for.

We was there by sunup every morning in our work clothes – me in overalls, long-sleeved shirt, high-top shoes, and canvas work gloves. Mommy didn't wear pants of any kind. I never understood how she could get so much work done in the long dresses she always wore. We started out with jackets, but after a couple of hours work, we'd be down to our shirtsleeves. Most days we worked 'til sundown, and we still had to haul the salvaged lumber to my place and unload it in the dark.

We was usually too focused on our work to notice the cars and trucks that went by. But a man in one car coming from Athens and turning the corner toward Cleveland ever day started blowing his horn when he passed. If our hands was free, we'd wave at him. Otherwise, we'd just nod in his direction.

One morning I was setting on a bench, taking a breakfast break. We had made cat-head biscuits which we'd split and filled with fried sausage. They was wrapped in brown paper and stuffed in a syrup bucket before we left home. After working for a couple of hours they tasted real good with a cup of black coffee from our thermos. The man that had been waving at us stopped his car and come over and flopped down beside me.

"I want to get yore name and her name," he said, pointing at my momma who was loading the boards we has just pulled down. "Are you two related?"

"I reckon we are. She's my momma."

"Well, I have a question for you."

He was making me kind of nervous. He was dressed in a suit and tie, and he looked like he might be some kind of government official. I was afraid he might say we wasn't permitted to tear down that building. What if he give us a big old fine we couldn't afford to pay?

"I been passing here twice a day for weeks," he said, "and I see two women taking this building down. I've never in my life seen women work so hard. What I want to know is, what do the men in this town do?"

I pointed across the street toward the courthouse where a hard ankle was setting on a bench under a shade tree. "You see that turkey perched on that bench over there? That's what they do. And it was probably a woman who built that bench." We both laughed about that.

It turned out he was a salesman who lived in Athens in McMinn County and worked in Cleveland in Bradley County. The shortest route was through Decatur in Meigs County. Me and Mommy was relieved he weren't no official after all, and we wasn't in trouble. We posed with our arms around each other's waist so he could take our picture, but we never even learnt his name.

While we was tearing that building down, we discovered there was a well in the middle. We didn't know what to do about that, so the man who owned the property hired a demolition crew out of Cleveland to come take it out. The feller who supervised them, a Mr. Johnson, would come over sometimes and watch us work and talk to us when we took a break. One day me and him walked over to the general grocery store across the street to get something for lunch. We picked up a box of saltine crackers and a couple of moon pies. The man at the meat counter wrapped us up some slices of cheese and baloney. The store owner was at the cash register. He put our things in a bag, and we paid him.

I didn't care for this man that owned the store cause he was always bad mouthing people who he thought was below him. I had heard him making fun of the workers taking out that well. He talked about one of them in particular, a young guy with a long pony tail, like he was a cross-eyed stepchild. As we was turning to walk out, he said, "We been watching all those workers over there at the courthouse, and we was wondering when you was gonna run off with that long-haired hippie on his motorcycle."

I turned around and glared at him. "There's more manhood in him," I said angrily, "than there is in the whole bunch you are stupid enough to pay to stand around in here all day long doing nothing."

He didn't have no quick reply to that, so we walked out the door. Mr. Johnson said, "Hazel, you done the right thing." He asked me to go with him back to the work site. He wanted me to hear it when he told his men, "I don't care if you have to drive to Athens or Cleveland or even Chattanooga for lunch, I don't want you to buy not one thing, not even a cigarette, from that store over there."

And none of them ever went back in there again. Sometimes when they was coming back to work, they'd yell out, "Hey, Hazel. We had a real good dinner down in Cleveland." I'd wave and smile, hoping that drag-ass man in that store seen that his big mouth had overloaded his hind end."

When we finally got finished tearing down that building in Decatur, I went to work building my house. Mommy helped me some, but I did most of it myself. I really liked building and felt real good at the end of ever day when I could see it was a little further along. I'd stand back and admire it, real proud-like.

I did hire a young boy to help me put the roof on my house. I really didn't like heights and had to will myself to climb up there. I liked to have some help to make things go faster so I could get back down to earth where I belonged. My helper was a scrawny little thing like me, but he was a good worker, and I liked helping him learn carpentry. One day a truck stopped out front and a man leaned out the window.

"Ain't you scared that little piece of trash on yore roof will blow off?" he asked. I guess he was trying to impress the other two men that was in his truck with him.

"There's more man on this roof," I yelled down, "than you and them other fellers in yore truck have got in yore britches all together. If I want to work with a little old boy, I will. It ain't none of yore business. So why don't you just get on down the road?"

I guess he didn't know what to say to that, so he moved on along. That little boy on my roof laughed, "I shore don't want you to get mad at me, Hazel!"

I never understood why some people think it makes them look important to tear somebody else down. But I'm like a bulldog when it comes to defending folks who ain't done nothing to nobody. The Lord don't pay you to abuse innocent people.

When I finished building my house, me and Dallas moved into it. Mommy was still living in the first one we built. Lurie was living in the trailer on my property. She had more kids now, and they was like chickens in a coop. Daniel was meaner than ever, but she still wouldn't leave him. One day he come home drunk, and her oldest boy, Leon, come running to get me.

"Aunt Hazel, Daddy's here, Daddy's here. He's got a gun and he's gonna kill us all. You gotta do something."

I told Leon to stay at my house with Dallas, and I took off for Lurie's trailer. She seen me coming and hollered for me to stay out.

"Don't come in here, Hazel. He's got a gun and he'll kill you, too."

"I'm coming in. I ain't scared of that son of a bitch."

Once inside I seen them huddled in a corner, and Lurie begging him not to kill them. He was setting on a chair holding a rifle pointed at them. I rushed over to where he was setting and before he knowed what was happening, I shoved the mouth of that rifle barrel into his leg and put my hand over his at the trigger.

"Come on, Dan," I sneered. "You want to shoot somebody? Let's see what it feels like to get shot."

"Stop it, Hazel," Lurie begged, still hovering in the corner. "Yore gonna blow his leg off."

"Shut up, Lurie. He wants somebody to get shot, else he wouldn't have this gun. Let him find out what it's like to be on the other end of that barrel."

"Hazel, don't pull that trigger," Dan begged. "I weren't gonna hurt nobody. I was just playing around." I could see he was really scared, and I was glad.

"Playing huh? It don't look like playing to me when you scare yore wife and kids half to death. I ought to blast yore leg off, you son of a bitch. Better yet, blow yore head off. Lurie and them young'uns'd be better off if you was dead."

By this time I'd wrangled the rifle away from him and had it pointed at his head. "No, Hazel, please don't shoot me. I'm sorry. I won't scare them no more."

"You get yore sorry ass off this property, and I don't want to see hide nor hair of you again."

He high tailed it out the door with Lurie calling after him, "It'll be all right, Dan. I know you didn't aim to harm us none. You sober up and come on back home, you hear?"

I looked at her with disgust. "People are always asking why I'm so mean, always fighting, when you and Mommy and Lena is so good. Well, I have to be mean and fight for all of us. Who else is gonna take care of you? Not the sorry ass men you put up with."

Mommy worried a lot over her children that was still living at home. One of my little sisters had started going off with boys, and when she was late coming home, Mommy would ask me to go look for her.

"Fireball," she'd say, "please go see if you can find her. I can't sleep 'til I know she's safe."

I had a friend, a neighbor guy named Clyde, who I'd wake up sometimes and get him to go with me looking for her. Most of the time we found her at a nearby lake where kids hung out, but one night we didn't find her there.

We was in Clyde's pickup truck, and we decided we better check out the restaurants and honkytonks where she might be. We went to the first one and went inside and looked around. We asked a few folks if they'd seen anybody there that looked like her, but nobody could help us. So we got back in the truck and checked out a few more places.

We drove all over everwhere looking for her, and we was about out of gas. When we stopped at a service station we heard somebody moaning. We looked in the bed of the truck and there she was, holding her stomach and saying she thought she was gonna throw up. She had been drinking at the first place we stopped and had went outside for some air. When she recognized Clyde's truck, she climbed in the back and passed out. We had drove all over two counties with her in the back of that dad burn truck the whole time.

CHAPTER 8:
OAK RIDGE BEFORE AMOS

When the government started building the bomb in Oak Ridge, about 60 or 70 miles north of Decatur, a lot of folks from Meigs County got on up there. Mr. Watson, the grocery store owner, had bought an old school bus to transport people back and forth. He helped farm hands who was good laborers get jobs in construction.

Since Mr. Watson liked me and had learnt what a good worker I was, he said, "Little Fireball, there's something big happening up there, and I think you should be a part of it. I'm gonna get you a job washing dishes in a restaurant in Oak Ridge."

"Oh, I don't think my momma will go up there, Mr. Watson."

"I know, Little Fireball. But you can go. You'll be paid good, and you can ride the bus up there for free. You'll be able to give yore momma some money, and maybe she won't have to work so hard to feed yore brothers and sisters."

"That sounds good, Mr. Watson, and I appreciate it. But I don't think I'm qualified. I heard they wanted educated folks up there, and I ain't never got but one year of schooling."

"You don't need no education to wash dishes. I wish I could get you on at the bomb factory, but yore supposed to have a high school diploma, a college diploma in some areas, to work there. But working any job up there will be a real good opportunity for your future. You'll go on and on. I guarantee you'll make it."

I hadn't never turned down no kind of work, and I figured washing dishes couldn't be nowhere near as hard as plowing fields and cutting cord wood. It would be an adventure, and it would sure help to have regular work that paid good. So I left Dallas with Mommy, joined the men waiting in front of the courthouse, and caught that bus to Oak Ridge. I was the only woman on the bus, but that didn't bother me none since I already knowed most of the men and had worked longside some of them. I was all excited and a little nervous about working where they was making the bomb.

I started out as a dishwasher in a little place called The Oak Terrace where the day laborers and bosses ate lunch. It was located in the Grove Center. I'd only been washing dishes for a week when the owner, Mr. Roscoe Stephens, seen me loading dishes off the tables, and he said, "Little girl, you don't need to be washing dishes. You ought to be a waitress." I told him I was just a sawmill gal from the country. I said I couldn't read real good, and I was afraid I would pour coffee on top of people's heads, but he just laughed and said I'd work out just fine. I didn't tell him that before I come to Oak Ridge, I hadn't never even eat in no restaurant. Back home I was always satisfied if everbody had a piece of cornbread.

I soon learnt waitressing work was easy. I didn't pour no coffee on nobody's head, so I relaxed and enjoyed it. I could remember orders real good, and I worked the cash register and made change real fast. Nobody would of believed I only went to school one year, and not ever day then. People liked me, and though I didn't know most of their names, I remembered faces real easy. Pretty soon a lot of the regulars become friends.

Oak Ridge was a mighty interesting place during those days. The whole town had been kept secret 'til not long before I went to work up there. Before the government let the workers – and the world – know what was really going on, it was called The Secret City. With 70,000 people working there, it weren't even on no map. People had to sign a paper saying they wouldn't talk about their work to nobody, not even their families. There was secret work going on in four different valleys, but the people living and working in one valley didn't even know the others was there. They was told it was all for the war effort, but now the war was over, and the atomic bomb had been dropped on Japan, so it weren't no secret no more.

Now Oak Ridge was building up so fast you couldn't keep up with all the changes. More people was coming and going, but they still had to wear badges and go through security checks cause the government still controlled everything. It would be a few more years before people could come and go there without going through a guard gate. Mud was a big problem, so they had put in wooden sidewalks, but in some areas you needed rubber boots to keep yore feet dry.

There was all these scientists walking around with their heads in a book. They was so important, if you was driving down the street and one walked out in front of you, you wasn't supposed to blow yore horn. You was supposed to just stop and let them cross and not say nothing, even if they got halfway across and just stood there. It's still a wonder some of them didn't get ran over.

And there was rules about how to deal with them in restaurants, and, I guess, other places, too. You was to take their order and be polite, but you wasn't to try to have conversation with them. You let them set where they wanted to, and if they wanted to stand up or even set on the floor, you was to leave them alone. And if they broke or spilled something, you was to clean it up without questions. If one come in and ordered something and then left without paying for it, you wasn't supposed to say nothing. After they left, you was supposed to call the police, and they'd go get yore money from the government.

Things was working out just fine for me in Oak Ridge. It shore was different from Decatur. I thought it was kind of exciting being where so much was happening, and a little bit scary because of the bomb. But the work was lots more easier and the pay more reliable than any work I ever done in Meigs County.

After a while my boss pulled some strings to get me a place in the Oak Ridge girls' dormitory that was supposed to be just for people who worked in the government facilities. This meant I wouldn't have to make that long ride back and forth every day, plus I could work some evenings when the tips was better.

Oak Ridge dormitories

So Mommy kept Dallas during the week, but on the weekends I spent my time with them, helping out at home and taking them places. I bought me a reliable car so I could come home whenever I had time off and didn't have to depend on the bus schedule. I could give Mommy money now, and like Mr. Watson said, she didn't have to get out and work so hard like before. She really hadn't wanted me to go to Oak Ridge cause she worried that with my temper, and her not there to tone it down, I'd get in trouble. But now that she seen that I was doing good, she didn't worry so much.

Dallas really loved his Granny Lamb, so he was a happy young'un. My only worry was that his Granny was spoiling him. I'd bring him little toys to play with, but not more than he needed. But his Granny tried to give him everthing he wanted. One time he was playing with a plastic toy she had got him, and he was being real rough kicking it around. I was gonna take it away from him. I said, "Mommy, he's gonna tear that up."

But Mommy said, "Oh, he ain't gonna hurt it. Let him enjoy it. You didn't get to have no play-purties when you was little."

"I weren't spoiled neither. A kid don't need to have ever little thing he wants," I answered. But I didn't take the toy away, and sure enough, he was rolling it around on the floor and kicked it and broke it. A spindle inside went flying out.

"I told you he'd break it," I said to Mommy.

"Come here, baby. Granny will make you a dancer out of that little piece that popped out."

I just shook my head. "He's gonna tear up everthing you got if you reward him when he breaks things." But I never broke her of spoiling him, and he turned out okay, so maybe I was being a little too particular.

I was looking down the road and begin saving money to buy some land to build me a house in Oak Ridge. Meanwhile, I liked living in the dormitory. It was real different from any place I'd lived before, since I had me a nice room all by myself. It was on the ground floor with a big window, so I got a lot of light. I had a comfortable bed, a chair, and a dresser to put my things in. The bathrooms was down at the end of the hall, but at least they was inside. There was a big cafeteria where we took our meals.

I missed my family, so I put pictures of my six sisters and three brothers on the wall facing the windows. I liked seeing them there when I woke up in the morning and again when I come in after a work shift.

My building just had women in it, but there was some dormitories where the women was on the bottom floor and men was on the upper floor. I heard there was a lot of visiting back and forth in those. There wasn't a lot of females working in the part of Oak Ridge where I was compared to all the soldiers and other men working there, so we got a lot of attention. There was some women soldiers, but a lot of the females I met was bookkeepers. I was the only girl dishwasher when I started out, but soon I got to work with other females who was waitresses.

Any time we women went outside, there was soldiers like a dadgum swarm of bees all over us. We almost needed a police escort to get from one place to the other. Sometimes we'd come home and there'd be so many men lined up on the porch we could hardly get inside. But I figured most of them probably had a wife and babies somewhere, so I didn't pay them no nevermind. Sometimes the Army would do raids on the female dorms cause soldiers wasn't supposed to be in women's rooms. An officer knocked on my door one night and asked if I had a man in there, I told him, "I don't sleep with soldiers."

The soldiers' barracks was behind our dormitory, so I had to be careful to keep my shade pulled down when I was changing my clothes. One weekend when I come back from visiting Dallas and Mommy in Decatur, I walked in my room and it looked like a hundred soldiers was staring in my window where I had left the shade up. That almost scared the water out of me. I run to the desk clerk and asked if she could tell me what was going on.

She was a real nice lady. She said, "I don't know, Hazel, but I'll see what I can find out."

I waited up front for her. I was too nervous to go back to my room. In a little while she come back laughing. "Hazel, you won't believe what them soldiers was doing. They was looking at them pictures you got hanging on yore wall. They said they never seen so many pretty women. They wanted to know who they was and where they could meet them."

That tickled me a lot. I couldn't wait to get back home and tell my sisters about all the commotion their pictures stirred up. But I got more careful about pulling my shade down from then on.

CHAPTER 9:
AMOS GIBBS

Amos Gibbs

I weren't looking for no boyfriend, but a hard ankle who worked in government transportation would come in the restaurant and flirt with me. His name was Amos Gibbs. He kept after me to go out with him, and even though he was real good looking with red hair and blue eyes, I said I weren't interested.

Me and Amos did become friends. We talked about our young'uns. He had four – a boy and three girls – who was living with his momma down in Ringold, Georgia. His wife had died a few years before when the last girl was born.

Amos would sometimes give me a ride, dropping me off in Decatur, when he was going down to his momma's to see his kids. One day he talked me into going on down to Georgia with him. Since I hadn't never been nowhere but Decatur and Oakridge, Tennessee, I thought it might be good to see some place different. So one Saturday we picked up Dallas from my momma's and drove on down.

When we got there we found his momma setting on the front porch holding little Andra Mae, the youngest of Amos's young'uns, on her lap. The other two girls, Sherry Ann and Patsy, was setting on the top step, and the boy, James Lewis – they called him Buddy, was playing mumblety peg with his pocket knife in the dirt yard. We joined his momma and the girls on the porch. Buddy, who was about eight years old, watched me suspiciously from a distance, not sure what this woman was doing with his daddy. The oldest girl, Sherry Ann, was about 12 years old. She was real sweet, but she didn't talk. She looked normal, but I could tell right off she weren't right. The other girl, Patsy, who was about 10 years old, seemed okay.

Amos's momma was real sweet, but she was in pore health and looked awful tired, and I knowed she weren't in no condition to give them kids a proper looking after. His daddy seemed all right at first, but I could tell Sherry Ann was scared of him. She acted real upset when he come near her. I suspected he had abused her, and later I found out that he had.

I couldn't hardly stand the way some others in his family treated Sherry Ann, neither. One of Amos's brothers bragged that when she didn't do what he said to do, he'd take her out on the porch, lean her over a chair, pull down her drawers and whip her ass. Even Buddy, her brother, said real mean things about her.

It didn't take long for Amos's momma to ask me wouldn't I marry him. "Hazel," she said, "these young'uns needs a momma. My health ain't good and I'm getting more bed-ridden day by day. My daughters help some, but they can't take care of them all the time. If you was to marry Amos, I know you'd be a good momma to them just like you are to yore Dallas.

"Well," I said, "I can see they need a momma, but I ain't ready to get married again. And taking on four step kids is a big decision when I ain't but nineteen years old myself."

Stepchildren Buddy, Andra Mae, Sherry Ann, and Patsy Gibbs

On the way home I told Amos I didn't like the way they treated Sherry Ann. He said it weren't none of my business and to keep out of it.

"Well, if they was my kids....," I began.

"Well, they ain't yore kids."

"But if they was...," I began again.

"Well, you know there's a solution to that," he said, meaning I could marry him.

I didn't tell Amos right away, but I decided then and there I was gonna have to marry him. He was 17 years older than me, and that seemed like a lot, but them kids, especially Sherry Ann, needed me, and I knowed I couldn't let them down.

When we talked about getting married, Amos said, "I don't keep my kids." He wanted to take the baby and leave the others with his momma, but I said, "No. We gonna take them all or we ain't taking none of them, which means I ain't marrying you."

I didn't say it out loud, but I reckoned from the get-go I was marrying them kids, not their daddy. And though I weren't turning back, a part of me wondered if I was making a big mistake.

We got married at the courthouse in Ringold cause they didn't have no three day waiting period like they had in Oak Ridge. When we got done, Amos said, "Let's go home."

"We ain't going nowhere," I said, "'til we pick up them young'uns at yore momma's."

Amos was renting a house on Taylor Road in the Marlow community near Oak Ridge. It was also called the Dosset area. The railroad run through Dosset tunnel, and lots of folks took the train from the Dosset Depot to Elza Gate where they would catch buses to their work places in Oakridge. Amos, like his daddy and brother Red, had worked for the L & N Railroad, but now he had started driving one of the buses that was transporting folks all over the place. He said at one time there was 800 buses running in Oak Ridge.

Marlow was a country community and there weren't much there. Brock's store was about the only place you could buy anything. There was a creek nearby, but in those days I didn't have no time for fishing.

When we got married, I moved out of the dormitory and in with Amos. But with me and Dallas and Amos and his four, it was pretty crowded. We couldn't hardly keep from stepping all over each other. I figured it was time to get busy building us a house. I had bought a piece of land not far from where we was living. I got it from Lawrence Smith who owned Smith's Coal Yard along with his daddy Theodore, who everybody called Poppy. Over the years, Poppy would become a real good friend to me.

I was still working at the Oak Terrace restaurant, but every minute I weren't working or sleeping I spent building that house. I cut down the trees and rented a tractor to grade the road leading in to where I was building it. I never had drove no tractor, so I had to teach myself how to operate it. I figured it out pretty quick, though, and got the grading done all by myself.

Amos weren't much help at all. He was working, driving a bus for the Y-12 plant at Oak Ridge, taking scientists from one place to the other. But at the end of the day, he wanted to rest. He weren't interested in helping build no house. His brother Vernon, come and stayed with us a while. We was even more crowded, but at least he was willing to help me some. Amos was real jealous and didn't trust him — and Vernon did try to get me to go to bed with him — so he run him off after a little while.

My brother Lonzo, who had been cripple and still didn't walk too good, wanted to help me with the house. I appreciated that he wanted to work, and I couldn't say no to him helping me out, but I worried he might get hurt. A building site ain't always safe. There's lots of things easy to trip over and sometimes you have to dodge stuff to keep it from falling on yore head. I tried to think of things he could do that wasn't too risky and wouldn't slow me down none neither.

Lonzo was pretty handy with a hammer and saw, so I could find things for him to do when I was working on the ground level. But one day I was up in the rafters laying in the ceiling and he wanted to come up there and help. I told him it weren't safe, but he kept pestering me, saying he was shore he could do it and he wouldn't fall. So I finally give in.

"If you can climb up here, I guess I can use some help."

He made it up there on the ladder and was having to stretch to step from beam to beam to get over to where I was. He kept saying, "I won't fall! I won't fall!"

I looked over just in time to see him miss a step and throw up his hands, scratching his arms as he fell between the rafters.

"Whack!" he landed on the floor.

I was praying he weren't dead.

"Lonzo," I shouted down through the rafters when I seen he was alive, "I ought to whip yore ass!"

"See. I told you I could do it," he grinned. I just shook my head. After that I kidded him about being a bird flying through the rafters.

I kept at it every minute I could squeeze in, and it weren't too long before I got that house finished and we moved in. It only had two rooms, and I was pregnant by that time, so we was still crowded, but we did have an attic where the kids could sleep. We built the outhouse out back

House in the Marlowe community after a kitchen was added on the back. More additions were made later.

and dug a well to draw water from. It would be a while before we'd get electricity, but we used kerosene lamps, and we split plenty of firewood and stove wood from the trees I had cut down.

By the time we moved into that house, I had bought another piece of land next to what I already had. It had an old house on it and I got busy fixing it up for Amos's momma. She was so happy to get to move up to Oak Ridge near Amos and the rest of us. She had whispered to me one time she felt safer when I was around, so I told his daddy he could come, too, but there weren't gonna be no bad behavior.

I couldn't say too much before, but things would be different if they was living on my land. Amos's sister had told me the old man would beat his wife, even after she was bedridden. One time, she said, she saw him hit her in the face with his fist while she was laying in the bed. And one of the kids told me, "Paw Paw whips Maw Maw any time he gets a mind to."

"If you ever hit her," I told him, "after I kick yore ass, you won't sleep another night in my house."

Amos didn't like me talking to his daddy like that, but I didn't care. It was my land and my house. If his daddy didn't like it, he could stay in Georgia. I'd seen my momma live with abuse, but now, in my own house and on my own property, I had some control. Weren't nobody gonna be mistreated as long as I was around.

I know I was meaner than hell when it come to protecting folks. Sometimes I wondered why God didn't just reach down and smack me in the mouth. But as far as I know, Mister Gibbs never hit his wife after they moved into that house. Miz Gibbs told me one time he was threatening her and she told him she was gonna tell Hazel on him, and he never bothered her again.

On July 19, 1952, when I was 21 years old, I give birth to a boy, a beautiful little blue-eyed blond-headed angel. He looked a lot like his daddy, who I thought was a still a good looking man. We named him Cecil Ferrell Gibbs, but we would come to call him Butch, a name that was give to him by a babysitter who we left him with one time but forgot to tell her his name. He was born at the old Dr. Stone Hospital in Oliver Springs. What should have been a happy day was a sad one, though, cause sweet Sherry Ann died of a brain tumor on the very day he was born.

A few years later, in 1955, we added a sweet little girl to the family. We named her Neomi. This time I went to the Oak Ridge hospital. And I remember the day we proudly brought her home through six inches of snow – a lot for where we lived – bundled up in a pretty pink blanket.

By this time Patsy had married and had a young'un of her own, but there was still seven of us sharing that house. It seemed like we was always bumping into each other, so we added another room. Later more rooms would be added to that house, but you could always tell which ones I built cause the ceilings was low enough for me to reach up to paint them without having to stand on nothing. I still didn't like heights.

Butch was three years old now, and he had got use to being the baby. I guess we had really spoiled him, so when Neomi was born he weren't too happy about it. When I would be nursing her, he'd sit real close to me, sucking his thumb and reaching across with the other hand to tug on the opposite ear. One day he was leaning in with his shoulder pushing into my breast.

"Set up, Butch. Yore gonna hurt the baby," I said, shifting her to the other breast.

"I'm gonna frow dat baby in duh yard," he muttered, not taking his thumb out of his mouth or letting go of his ear.

Amos holding Butch, Hazel holding Neomi

"Why, Butch, don't you like yore baby sister? Do you wish she was a boy?"

"A boy ud be better'n a durn girl," he replied.

That give me an idea. I made up a little song that I'd sing to Butch. I think it made him feel more special to have a song that took his side of things. Later I sang it to Neomi, too, when she was little. It went like this:

Through a nursery creeping, a little boy came peeping
Gaily peeping through a golden curl.
Add a little bundle, such a funny bundle.
It was a tiny little baby girl.

She came to town that morning as the day was dawning.
Mother thought it'd fill his heart with joy.
But he shook his little head and to his mother said,
Gee I wish you had bought a boy.

Can't you take it back and change it for another?
I don't want no baby sister don't you see?
I'd rather have a little baby brother
To play a game of ball with me.

Oh, it aint no fun to play with dolls and such things.
A girl, you know, could never fix a toy.
I'll tell you what to do, if it's the same with you,
We'll take it back and change it for a boy.

Momma, ain't it awfully funny?
Did it cost a lot of money?
Won't it be an awful lot of care?

It aint a good one mother.
You'll have to get another.
Lord, can't you see it hasn't any hair?

Don't its teeth come with it?
Will its nose grow, will it?
Won't it be an awful lot of care?

I'll tell you what to do,
If it's the same with you.
We'll take it back and change it for a boy.

Another song Neomi liked for me to sing was "Buffalo Girl." She
liked the part that went. "Gonna dance with the dolly with a hole in her

Hazel and Butch

Butch Gibbs

stocking, and her knees keep a knocking, and her toes keep a rocking."
And there was a sad song I wrote that she was always wanting me to
sing, too. It was about a drunk driver who ran over two kids.

It went like this:

Now listen you drunken driver, while here on earth you dwell,
You'll never know when the time will come you'll have to say farewell,
To your dear old mother and father, though they may be miles away
So don't be drinking whiskey while driving on your way.

I saw an accident one day
That would charm the heart of man
And teach him not to drink a drop
While the steering wheel's in his hand.

This drunk man saw these two dear kids
And he uttered a drunken sound
Get out of the road you little fools
And the car it brought them down.

The driver struck the little girl
Taken her like away
And the little boy in a gore of blood
In the ditch lying there did lay.

My marriage to Amos was not easy, but it was my longest one. I knowed Amos cheated on me, but I stayed because he was rough on the kids, and I knowed I couldn't leave them unprotected. "Amos," I'd say, "you don't have to beat kids to teach them right from wrong. And if yore gonna cuss, take it out to the corn crib where they can't hear you."

But he didn't listen. He threatened that he'd keep them all, including Neomi and Butch, if I left. He'd stand Neomi in the hall and say, "Hazel, you know you can't leave this purty little thing."

"You son of a bitch, you know you've got me trapped," I said. Unhappy as I was with Amos, I knowed my kids was worth it.

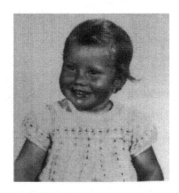

Neomi Gibbs

So I stayed. When Amos would get mad, they knowed it was "Katy barred the door," and them kids would scatter like rats, running different directions to hide. Sometimes he'd line them up for a whipping, and they'd holler for me to come talk to him. There was times when I thought they needed a switching, but before Sherry Ann died, I told him he better not never lay a hand on her. She was so innocent, and if she followed the others in getting into mischief, it was cause she didn't know no better. I weren't gonna let nobody mistreat her the way they done before I come into the picture.

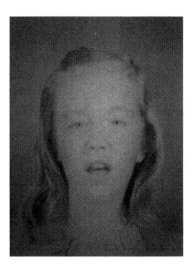

Sherry Ann Gibbs

Sherry Ann never was able to talk, but she tried. She would say "Murrr, Murr" and I knowed she was trying to say, "Mother."

And I told her, "Honey, you don't have to worry as long as Mother is here. I'm not gonna let nobody hurt you."

Amos had to mouth off, "I'll whip her ass when I want to."

"For the protection of yore ass," I said, "you might want to think about it." I had been protecting folks all my life, and I weren't gonna stop now.

Dallas got along just fine with his step brother and sisters, but Amos weren't easy on him, and I had to step in sometimes. So I let him spend a lot of time down in Decatur with my momma, his Granny Lamb. They was still real close. I had offered to build Mommy a house by me if she would move up to Oak Ridge, but she wanted to stay in Meigs County where most of my brothers and sisters was living.

Buddy didn't mind working and was a big help in the garden. We was the same size, even wore each other's overalls. But it was clear he hadn't had a lot of discipline, so I had to take a firm hand with him. His daddy didn't like me doing that. It was my belief that the woman ought to be in charge of teaching the girls to do right and the daddy ought to be responsible for the boys. But I didn't think Amos was strict enough with Buddy though he was too rough on Dallas and sometimes with Butch.

Dallas Ricker, Neomi and Butch Gibbs

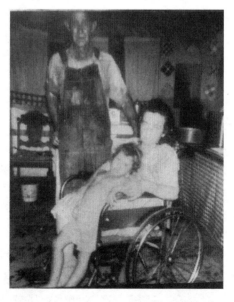

Neomi with her Gibbs grandparents

Buddy, big as he was, still peed in the bed. I was getting tired of going up to the loft and changing his sheets and lugging that bedding downstairs to be washed ever day. I wanted Amos to talk to him about it, but he wouldn't. I believed Buddy was just too lazy to get up and come downstairs and go to the outhouse.

One night me and Amos was setting in the living room listening to the radio when a stream of liquid begin to run across the ceiling near the edge of the wall. It dripped down, landing on Amos's bald spot. "What in the hell is that?" he shouted.

"That's Buddy upstairs peeing," I said.

Amos – cussing and rubbing his head – raced up the stairs. "I'll break his damned head..."

Buddy, had circled the loft to stay out of Amos's reached. Now he run downstairs shouting, "He's gonna whip me. He's gonna whip me."

"No, he's not gonna whip you," I said. But from now on, you go to the toilet before you go to bed or I'm the one what's gonna whip you."

It's a good thing we put an end to that, cause Buddy ended up having a successful military career. He served five tours of duty in Vietnam in the sixties and seventies with the 101st Airborne Screaming Eagles. But they wouldn't have took him in the Army if he was still wetting the bed when he went to enlist.

I was always busy, working in the garden and raising animals. I had learnt from Boyd growing up that hogs was the quickest way to get a turn around on money spent raising animals. I could get slop to feed them from the restaurant where I worked and from a few others places, as well.

Neomi always liked to go with us to the Oak Terrace restaurant to get the leftover table scraps and any fruits and vegetables that had gone bad. She never liked to stay home with just her brothers cause they would devil the life out of her. And the black woman who was in charge of separating out the bad produce for the hogs liked Neomi and would slip a good apple or orange for her in a box of wilted, rotting lettuce.

Poppy Smith was a good neighbor and also a big help with the hogs. He lived across the hill and owned all the land around ours. I had bought some of my 18 acres, one bump at a time, from his son. Poppy really loved Neomi and always had an apple in his overall pocket for her ever time he come around. I guess between him and that woman at Oak Terrace she got plenty of fresh fruit.

One day I was looking through the local newspaper and I saw an ad for Olan Mills Studios. It had a coupon that said "Free black and white eight-by-ten portrait." I decided to go have my picture made. I combed my hair and put on some pretty red lipstick. I didn't even change out of my waitress uniform. I went straight there from work. They took my picture and said it would be ready in one week. Imagine my surprise when I went to pick it up. There in the front window was a great big colored picture of me. I was amazed by that. I didn't have no money for no extra copies of the black and white picture, much less that big old colored one. But I was kinda proud they thought I was pretty enough to be in the front window.

Hazel, Olan Mills portrait

In 1959 they had a big celebration on the ten-year anniversary of the opening of Oak Ridge to the outside world. They had a big parade and we took the kids and went to see it. It really brought back memories, especially when I seen a car with a sign in the window that said "dormitory resident." A lot had happened in the last nine years. I thought about how I didn't know nothing when I first arrived to this strange place that was like another world to a little country gal who hadn't never been no "let's go to town" girl.

Sometime in the fifties we'd bought out first television. It was a used black and white set, and we paid $15 for it, making payments over time. We couldn't get but one channel. It was out of Knoxville. Tired as I was at the end of a long day, after the kids was in bed, I couldn't resist setting up and watching whatever was on that one station 'til it signed off at midnight with "The Star Spangled Banner" playing. I liked that music a lot, so I always listened to the very last note before I turned it off.

Mornings, while the kids was eating breakfast and getting dressed to go to school, we would watch the Cas Walker Farm and Home Show on television. We had been listening to that show on the radio for years before we got a T.V. set. We had listened to, and now watched, Dolly Parton, who had been singing on the Cas Walker show since she was just ten years old, a long time before she made it big in Nashville. And the Everly Brothers was regulars on there, too. I thought they was real handsome, and they sung real pretty.

Cas Walker owned a string of grocery stores in and around Knoxville and he advertised them on his variety show. There weren't one near us, so we usually bought our groceries at the IGA store near Elza Gate. Amos liked to tease the owner there, calling him "Little Cas."

Neomi liked singing a jingle that two little black boys eating watermelon sang on the show:

> *Thumping good, thumping good,*
> *Cas Walker melons are thumping good,*
> *Red, ripe, and ready to eat.*
> *Cold, delicious, and so sweet*
> *Cas Walker melons can't be beat.*
> *Cas Walker melons are thumping good*

Cas was a politician as well as a businessman and T.V. show sponsor and announcer. I met him some years later when the show was broadcast out of Ciderville Music Barn where I would sing and dance. He was a big mess and there was all kinds of stories about his outlandish stunts. David West, who played banjo on Cas's show and later owned Ciderville, thought real highly of him and said he learnt a lot about operating a successful business from Cas. But I heard that somebody who didn't like him said one time if you ordered a whole truckload of bastards and all they sent you was Cas Walker, you'd feel like you got your money's worth.

I didn't whup my kids much, but I did give my stepson Buddy a switching when he was 17 years old, the day before he joined the Army. I was working two shifts at the restaurant and trying to get a little rest between them. When I got home that day, Neomi, met me at the door a crying.

"Buddy whupped me while you was working," she snuffled.

"Buddy, did you whup yore little sister?" I asked.

"I shore did, and I'll do it again," he boasted.

"You will, will you?"

"Yeah. I'll get a switch and tear up her tail."

"Shoot yore mouth off like that one more time, and I don't care if you are nearly a grown up man, I'm gonna whup yore behind."

"You ain't gonna try to whup me," he laughed.

"No, I ain't gonna try," I replied.

Well, he was laughing on the other side of his face when I got a switch and whupped him good.

The next day we said good-bye and he was off to boot camp. He weren't a bad boy, but he had got in a fist fight with the son of a judge. When he went to court the judge give him a choice, jail or the army. He took the army. We didn't see him real often after that, but he called me a lot and was always telling me I ought to leave his daddy. He knowed how mean Amos could be and that he cheated on me. I don't know if he was aware that his daddy had even slept with one of my own sisters. I couldn't forgive Amos or her for that.

Much as I wanted to, I couldn't leave yet. "You know I can't leave these babies, Buddy. I'll have to stay 'til they are all growed up."

But the day the youngest step girl, Andra Mae, got married, I called Buddy up and said, "Yore little sister just walked out the door with her new husband, and I am leaving yore daddy."

"Well, it's about time. What are you gonna do now?

"Well, I ain't quite shore. I don't really have no plan."

"Then why don't you come down here and see me."

He was stationed at Fort Benning, Georgia. I thought visiting him was a good idea. I was ready for little bit of enjoyment, so I went. He offered to come get me, but I said no, I'd try to make it by myself. I'd never drove that far before, and I was anxious about it, but I made it. I did stop and call him up ever time I found a place that had a telephone.

I wanted to make sure I was on the right road, so it took me all day to get there.

It was real good to see Buddy again. We had parties, and I played the guitar and sang for him and his friends. When he introduced me to his buddies, he laughed and told them, "You see that wormy little old woman? She whipped my butt the day before I joined the Army."

"Now, tell them why I done it."

"I was being a smart ass," he replied. "She was so little she had to look up to see my face. But she whipped me just the same."

They loved beating him to death with teasing. They'd say to me, "Let us watch you whip his butt!" We'd all have a good laugh. But he also made it known that he loved me and if it hadn't been for me he'd probably be in prison.

Hazel and stepson Buddy, Knoxville Fair, 1960

Buddy wanted me to stay in Georgia, but much as I wanted to, I couldn't leave Amos just yet. I had my kids to think about, so I went back to Oak Ridge and would stay with Amos for a few more years. This was a busy time for me, working at the restaurant, raising hogs, taking care of young'uns, and always building something. My sister Geraldine and her husband, Fred Childs, had moved to Oak Ridge not far from us so she could help babysit. I don't know what I'd a done without her.

I liked waiting tables and I was getting a good education about how a restaurant was run. The owner seen I was quick to learn, and he give me more and more responsibilities like ordering supplies and keeping records. In 1962 I decided I'd like to have my own place, so I bought a little piece of property and got busy laying the foundation for Hazel's Grill. Somebody asked Dallas why I named it that, and he said, "Cause momma can't spell restaurant."

Some folks thought I wouldn't be able to make no go of it, running my own restaurant. They said folks in Oak Ridge was sophisticated and wouldn't eat no country cooking like I was planning.

"Well," I said, "if they don't like what I serve, I'll take it home and feed it to the hogs. I know they'll eat it."

They said I'd go into debt and lose everthing I had, said I'd be broke in no time. But them naysayers was wrong. I may have been as country as turnip greens myself, not classy like my customers, but they couldn't get enough of my fresh eggs and homemade biscuits and sausage gravy. And the beef and the pork we raised and butchered was real popular, too. Lots of folks, after eating in my restaurant and seeing how good it was, would order a ham or a side of pork — even a whole hog – for their freezer.

I raised all kinds of vegetables, too, that we served fresh. And I had a whole big field of strawberries that I used to make desserts that everbody just loved. I guess by now my sisters seen that I could do more than boil water without spilling it!

We had a jukebox at Hazel's Grill. It was a big old floor model, and people would put in their ten cents for one or a quarter for three selections. Elvis Presley was real big then, so we heard him sing a lot, especially when teenagers come in. Roy Orbison and Patsy Cline was real popular, too. Butch and Neomi would pester me for a dime so they could watch through the glass as the arm picked up the record they chose and put it on the turn table. They was there so much, they got real good at dancing to the music from that jukebox. Pretty soon people was noticing this cute little boy with blue eyes and curly blond hair dancing with his pretty little dark-haired sister in her skirts held out with the stiff crinolines that was so stylish then. Folks would clap their hands for them when they was jitterbugging or doing the twist. Some people would buy them a Coca Cola or even give them a dime or a quarter for the entertainment. I didn't have no time for dancing, myself, but I was glad they was having a good time and didn't mind having to come to the restaurant after school ever afternoon.

There's a whole lot to do besides cooking and waiting on customers in a restaurant. I had to come in early, after slopping the hogs and getting the kids off to school, and get ready for the breakfast customers. Daily lunch specials changed based on what we had plenty of, so lots of days I had to get out the old typewriter I'd picked up somewhere and type up copies of the menu. This took a while cause there wasn't no copying machines back then, at least not none I could afford. I had to remove the old menus and slide the new ones inside the plastic covers that had "Hazel's Grill" on them.

And after we closed for the night, we still had cleaning up and things to do to get ready for the next day. I had to empty the cash registers, count the money and get the bank deposit ready. I was pretty tired by the time I got home, and we still had to slop the hogs again and pick vegetables for the next day.

Amos weren't no help in the restaurant. In fact, he made things harder. He'd come in and set there glaring at the men he thought was flirting with me. He threatened to shoot one of them, and I said, "Go ahead. Then they will come and arrest yore ass, and I won't have to put up with you running off my customers."

Me and Amos was both real firey. His family was Irish from Hayesville, North Carolina, and had helped with the Cherokee removal there. Me being part Cherokee, I guess it's no wonder we fought.

Menu cover

I met a lot of weird characters in my restaurant. We had one regular who come in every morning and asked for a cup of coffee. He always set down by the window. I'd bring him a cup of coffee and a glass of water. He'd set there a reading'til closing time, and then he'd leave a dollar bill on the table and start toward the door without never even touching that cup of coffee. I'd say, "Thank you," and sometimes he'd say, "Bye." That was all the conversation we ever had. I wonder if he might have been a famous scientist and I never realized it.

I made some good friends during this time. One was named Joyce Kidwell, and another was Stella Brock, who done my hair. Me and Hazel McMillan, who worked in my restaurant, was also good buddies. Folk kidded us, calling us the two mean Hazels. But my very best friend was my sister Geraldine. Geraldine was tall like our momma. Sometimes I called her Olive Oil, and we also called each other "Dummy." Her boy Joe and my Butch was about the same age and they was best of friends, too. Me and Geraldine both loved to sing. Sometimes we'd pile all the kids in the car — her baby Susan in front with us, the rest in the back

— and take off to see their granny, singing all the way to Decatur.

One time Geraldine and Fred wanted to plant a garden. They had a plow but they didn't have no mule. So they done what folks do during hard times. Fred agreed to pull the plow while Geraldine guided it down the furrows. I reckon she weren't doing it to Fred's satisfaction, cause he kept fussing at her. Finally she said, "Just let me pull the damn plow and you guide it."

A neighbor passed by while Geraldine was pulling that plow, and he was real surprised. The word got back to her that he had told a neighbor, "I seen something today I ain't never seen before. A man was a plowing with his wife hooked up to the plow!"

Amos had a good income, and now I was bringing home a good bit from the restaurant, too, so we didn't have no big financial worries, which was nice. That Christmas, we got the kids just about everthing they asked for. I really felt rich but also cautious, cause you never know what kind of turns life will take.

Neomi had seen commercials for the new Chatty Cathy doll on television, and that was at the top of her list. On Christmas Eve she was so excited, I couldn't get her to go to bed. She kept begging to stay up a little bit longer to watch one more Christmas show on television. Dallas told her Santa Claus weren't gonna come if she didn't go to bed, but she didn't believe him.

On Christmas morning when she come downstairs, Dallas was setting on a brand new bicycle, holding a doll in his arms like he was real proud of it. He told Neomi Santa Claus left it for him. He said Santa was so tired of waiting for her to go to bed, he couldn't remember who the doll was for and put Dallas' name on it instead of hers. She started hollering for me saying Dallas had her Chatty Cathy. I told him he had tormented her enough, and I made him give it to her. We was all real happy the rest of that day, Neomi playing with her doll and the boys riding that bike and playing cowboys with their new six shooters.

CHAPTER 10:
ELMER SEIVERS AND GRADY TRUETT

Elmer and Hazel Seivers

In 1963 I left Amos. He claimed I left him for a grease monkey. Elmer Seivers was a mechanic at a local Gulf Station in Oak Ridge, and it's true, me and him did get together before I divorced Amos, but I'd decided long before I ever met Elmer I was gonna leave Amos.

I told Amos, "Ever time I turned around, you was always saying I was a cheating, so I figured I'd better do it to keep you from going to hell for lying."

When me and Elmer got together I sold my restaurant, and we moved to Columbus, Georgia. He was going through a divorce, too, so it would be a while before we could get married. Although I left Amos in sixty-three, me and Elmer didn't tie the knot 'til May 17, 1965.

The hardest part of the move to Georgia was that I decided to leave Neomi in Oak Ridge. She was 8 years old, smart, and doing good in school. Me and Amos worked out a plan of joint custody of her and Butch. He was supposed to have them one year then me the next. But I weren't shore I would be in a stable situation, and I didn't want her to be drug from one place to another and get behind in school.

I told Amos he could live in the house, which was mine, and look after Neomi if he would pay the real estate taxes. He always petted Neomi, so I weren't afraid he would mistreat her. And since my sister Geraldine lived nearby, I was shore she'd keep an eye on her for me. Neomi and her "Aunt Gerley" was real close. And Neomi loved her daddy. I told her one time, "Only you and God could love that man, and I'm not so sure about God." He could be hateful, but he did take good care of his little girl. She had to wear dresses to school, so Amos paid Geraldine ten cents apiece to iron them. I'm shore she always looked real pretty.

Dallas moved to Columbus with me. Butch, since him and Amos didn't get along so good, was back and forth between Georgia and Tennessee a lot. Neomi spent summers with me, and I shore missed her when she had to go back to Oak Ridge when school started.

She wrote me a letter one time saying she missed me so much and she cried for me at night. It just broke my heart, but I felt like I was doing what I had to do. And I was pretty shore her daddy put her up to writing that letter since he hadn't stopped trying to get me to come back to him. I kept that reminder that she loved and needed me in my billfold for years.

The first Christmas after I left Amos, he took the kid's to my step-daughter Patsy's house in Chattanooga, hoping to hide them from me.

But I found out about it, and me and Elmer went to her house to get them. Amos weren't too happy to see me with Elmer. He raised a ruckus and hit Elmer in the jaw with his fist. I told him to back off, and I took them kids with me.

I give Neomi fifty dollars that Christmas and she was real generous with it. She bought tickets for all four of Patsy's kids and herself to ride the Incline Railroad at Lookout Mountain. I was real proud of her for sharing like that.

Amos proved to be as ornery as I expected him to be about the taxes. When they come due, he didn't pay them. Every year I had to go back up there and raise Cain 'til he took care of it. Neomi said he just done that to get to see me. But she trusted him more than I did. I suspected he hoped if we defaulted on paying them taxes, he could sneak around and pay them and get the house in his name.

Years later, when Neomi was divorcing her first husband, she said Amos told her, "No way you could love him more than I loved yore momma, and I learnt to live without her." Later when I moved back up there and into a house near Neomi, he would pass my house on his way to see her. Even though he had got married again, if there was a car in my driveway, he'd ask Neomi, "Who's that son of a bitch up at yore momma's house?"

Elmer was good to me and my young'uns. He took me and Butch and Neomi on a trip all the way to Florida. I hadn't never been nowhere but Tennessee and Georgia, so this was like a trip to another world. We stayed in a motel, something I never had did before. I seen plants and animals that wasn't like any I'd ever saw, and the ocean with them big old waves was plumb amazing.

We went to Silver Springs and rode in a glass-bottom boat and seen a whole bunch of pretty fishes. They was all different colors and was prettier than anything I'd ever saw in a Tennessee creek or river. And they was so graceful. Some of them swimmed in little groups that the guide on the boat said was called "schools." I joked that some of them fish had more education than me.

We also went to the Six Gun Territory and seen covered wagons, teepees, and a big old iron train with a steam engine. We watched a pretend gun fight. Some of the actors who played like they was having a shootout let Neomi have her picture took with them afterwards. That really tickled her.

I don't remember what we fought about, but me and Elmer did have our battles. He had had a heart attack, and Neomi, who liked him a whole lot, was afraid I'd give him another one. And I'm not shore why we split up. I know it was my idea, so he must of did something I didn't like. Every time a man got shitty with me I wanted to do to him what I couldn't do to my daddy. I told all my husbands right from the get-go I didn't give no second chances, so he had been warned.

I didn't whip my kids much, but that don't mean they didn't do things sometimes that really got my goat. When they was little we lived in the country, so they coudn't get into the kinds of mischief there that was possible in a city like Columbus. Butch and Dallas was really pushing their limits, but Neomi loved to tattle and was always hoping they'd get a whipping, so I don't think they got by with much.

One time they used up a whole can of Elmer's shaving cream to fill up balloons. They thought it was fun throwing them at each other and watching them splash on the sidewalk when they dropped them. But when Elmer went to shave and the can was empty, it made him pretty mad.

Another time. they decided it would be fun to throw balloons full of water at passing cars. A man who got hit in the head with one of them chased Dallas and Butch up on the roof. Neomi, of course, saw it all and gave her report of what happened. I didn't whip them. I made it clear, though, that there weren't gonna be no more of that kind of behavior. I had learnt there was better ways to teach kids to behave than whipping them all the time. And, as far as I'm aware, they never threw no more water balloons at cars, at least not when Neomi was around to tattle on them.

I got a job waiting tables at a restaurant called Bugaloo's Barbecue and Pancake House. It was an eat-in and drive-through place, and we was always real busy. One time I come home from working a hard shift, tired and just wanting to rest a little. I couldn't believe what I seen when I opened the door. Them rascals had got into a pillow fight, and when one of the pillows busted open, they decided to throw feathers everwhere, pretending like it was snowing. And then somebody – I think it might have been Neomi this time – got the idea to get the can of flour out of the kitchen and throw that around, too.

I was so mad when I seen that mess. I got me a switch and I sat down on a chair, and I told them they was to clean up ever feather and ever speck of flour or they was gonna get a switching. They grumbled and complained ever time they thought they was finished and I'd point out one more feather or a patch of flour they had missed. But I didn't let them stop 'til ever speck was cleaned up. I still shake my head when I think about that. The things young'uns can come up with!

* * *

Grady Truett

My fourth husband was Grady Truett. He come and went pretty fast, so there's not much to tell there. He owned a car lot in Columbus. He drove a real pretty green Lincoln Continental. We married during the school year, and he didn't get to stick around long enough to meet Neomi, but she remembers me driving that Lincoln up to Oak Ridge. She was real taken with the head lights. They was hid behind little doors that opened when you turned the light switch on, and they'd pop out and rise up. Then when you turned them off they'd go back underneath and them little doors would close up. Neomi got a real kick out of that.

Like with most of my husbands after him, me and Truett met at a country jubilee where I was singing and dancing, spending as much time as I could entertaining little kids. A lot of their daddies was at war in Vietnam, where Buddy had also been sent. Their mommas looked so sad. Some of them told me they was having a hard time making ends meet on the allotment money they got. They wanted to get jobs, but with so many women looking for work, it was hard to find one. I hoped my guitar playing and singing and dancing cheered them up a little bit.

Chapter 11:
Lt Colonel Bill Williams

Lt Colonel Bill Williams

I met my third Georgia husband, my fifth one, in all, at a jubilee. His name was Bill Williams, and he was an Army Lieutenant Colonel. He was tall and well built, and I thought he looked real handsome in his uniform. He had lived all over the world and was more educated than other men I'd gone out with, so I was kind of surprised when he took a shine to this little country gal. When he first asked me to marry him, I said I'd have to think about it. Some woman told me I needed to make up my mind, cause there was several other women waiting their chance if I didn't want him. They seemed to think that catching a high-ranking officer like a colonel was a big deal, but to me he weren't no more special than any other man.

But Bill was real crazy about me. He wrote me love letters all the time, and I guess I just couldn't resist him. I didn't know nothing about the military life, but it didn't take me long to figure out I weren't cut out to be no officer's wife. We was supposed to go to highfaluting military parties and ceremonies, but I didn't like doing that, so I didn't go very much. I wouldn't put on airs like was expected of me. I just couldn't be nothing but what I was, plain and simple.

I despised going to buy groceries cause the soldiers would be all lined up around the commissary, and they'd salute me. I weren't no soldier, and I didn't think I was no different from other folks, so I didn't want them to do that. And some of them would point at me and say, "That there's the Colonel's wife," and they'd want to take my picture. Some folks said they wanted my picture cause I was pretty, but I kind of felt like they was making fun of me. So most of the time I made Bill go buy what we needed.

The Colonel was usually real good to me. If I seen something in a store window like a pretty blouse or jacket and said I liked it, he'd set me down somewhere and go back and buy it. When we got home he'd surprise me with it. But he couldn't just give it to me and let me enjoy it. One time he bought me a new wrist watch. He watched me open it, and said, "Now, be real careful with it. I know how careless you can be."

I bounced that watch off the wall. I told him, "If you give somebody a gift, you don't tell them how to use it. That takes all the joy out of it."

The colonel didn't want me to work, so I didn't have no job. That was kind of nice for a little while since I had worked so hard all my life. I could watch T.V. and read movie magazines, but that got boring real fast.

Plus, I never had to ask nobody for money before. Bill had been living in a house on the base at Fort Benning before we was married, but now he'd moved into my house with me and Butch. (Dallas had married and was living on his own by now.) But even though we was living in my house, I felt like he thought he had bought me. And it made me feel like a little kid having to ask for everthing.

I told him, "Becoming a military colonel didn't make you God. Yore not my owner and I don't have to jump ever time you point yore finger."

"You are taking it too seriously," he replied.

"Well, how many times am I gonna have to tell you a marriage license ain't no boss's papers?" I was about ready to tell him what I had told other husbands, "Get it right or get it gone."

Since I didn't live on the base and didn't hardly ever go to the parties and ceremonies Bill had to go to, I didn't make friends with any other officers' wives. So I never had nobody to talk to about how hard it was. Much as I tried to avoid it, sometimes I felt like I couldn't do nothing without the military having a say in it. I told Bill, "I'm gonna build me an outdoor toilet so I have something the government's not got its foot in."

I knowed things couldn't continue the way they was, so I was real happy when the colonel decided it was time to retire. I was missing my momma a lot and worried about how she was getting along in Meigs County, Tennessee, with me so far away in Georgia. So I convinced the colonel we should move back to where I growed up. This would put me nearer to Neomi, too, and I was wanting to have more time with her.

I had always kept my own place when I married. I didn't like moving in where another wife had been, and I didn't want to kiss nobody's shoes in order to have my kids with me. But me and Bill bought a red brick house together in Decatur. I did add on some rooms in the back after we had lived there a little while.

Bill got on with Meigs County as a deputy sheriff. I liked that I didn't have to deal with being seen as the Colonel's wife no more, but he still wanted to tell me what to do and how to act. And I still didn't like taking no orders. I guess that's why I didn't stick around very long with most of my husbands.

One day I was feeling kind of antsy, and I asked Bill for the car keys so I could go for a ride. He looked up from where he was setting in his easy chair reading *Time* magazine. "What do you want the car keys for, Hazel?" he asked.

"I want to go breathe some air that you ain't breathing," I replied.

"If you want the keys, ask me like a lady."

"You telling me I gotta say please?"

"Yes, M'am, that's what I'm saying."

"Well, I ain't no prisoner and I ain't one of yore dang soldiers. I don't beg for no permission. Just give me the damn car keys."

He just shook his head and handed me the keys. Bill never could resist giving me what I wanted for long.

Since I never did get to go to school when I was little, I made sure that my kids went. I hoped wouldn't none of them ever have to work as hard as I done growing up. So I tried to make sure they got a good education. Since Neomi liked school, I didn't need to worry about her none. And I thought Butch was going regular until I found out he was sneaking off to the store with some of his cousins and skipping school. When I asked him why, he said some of the kids was mean to him and he was afraid he'd get in a fight.

"I'll tell you what," I said, "I'll go to school with you and if anybody bothers you, I'll whup them. You know, I didn't get to go to school much, so I don't know exactly how to act. I can get on the bus okay, but when we get there, you may have to hold my hand and show me where to sit and what to do."

"Naw, you don't have to do that," Butch was quick to reply. "I think I can take care of myself. I know you have too much to do to go to school with me."

"Oh, I don't mind. I might learn something, and I'd like that a lot. But you may have to explain some things to me."

"Let me try it by myself tomorrow, and I'll let you know if them boys pester me."

Butch got up and went to school the next day, and the subject never come up again.

Butch

I got interested in another man in Decatur named Bill Wilkerson, so I decided it was time to divorce the Colonel. When we went to court, Judge Bill McKenzie was presiding. He asked me, "What did he do?"

I said, "Everthing."

"What do you mean?

"Well, he cleans the house and washes the clothes and cooks the meals."

"And you want to divorce him? You know you won't find another husband who'll do all that, don't you?"

"I reckon I won't. But I still want a divorce. He may be as handy as a pocket on a shirt, but it torques my jaw when he tries to make me act lady-like."

The judge just shook his head "I'm gonna give you this divorce, but it's the last one you'll get from this court as long as I live."

Well, I divorced one Bill that morning and married another Bill that afternoon. And little did anyone know that when me and the next one split up Judge McKenzie would be dead. So he was right. I didn't get another divorce in his court.

The Colonel moved away from Decatur pretty soon after the divorce. He said he couldn't bear being in the town where I was living with another man. He said I could keep the house, so I did. Some old gal told me, "I knowed a man like that wouldn't put up with a woman like you."

I told her, "I was the one that got the divorce, not him." That would be true of all my husbands. Not a one ever left me unless he died.

CHAPTER 12:
BILL WILKERSON

I died one time and my momma brought me back to life. I had married my sixth husband. He was a redneck clod-kicker from Decatur who I'll call Bill Wilkerson, although that's not his real name. I guess I thought he was gonna be a good one cause he was a Sunday School superintendent. He was at that Baptist church ever time the doors flew open. But our marriage was pretty rocky from the start.

Bill made me real mad one time, and I got the rifle and was gonna shoot him, but I couldn't find no bullets. His son Buddy lived in an apartment I'd added on to the back of my house when I was living there with the Colonel. I asked him if he had any cartridges, but he wouldn't give me none. So I went out in the yard and beat the windows out of Bill's truck – and him a setting in it – with the butt of my rifle. We lived next door to Sheriff Womack, but he didn't come out to see what was going on. Maybe he weren't home, or maybe when he heard the commotion he just shook his head and said, "Oh, that's just Hazel and her tomfoolery."

Bill was so mad. He couldn't believe what I done to his truck. He said he weren't staying with no crazy woman; he was moving out. It was in the summer, and Neomi was with us. She got real upset when she seen him rolling out the only T.V. set we had. She tried to protest, but I said, "Let him take whatever he thinks is his so long as he gets the hell outta here."

"Well, if I ever get married and divorced," Neomi said, "I'm taking everything except his clothes that I can't wear."

But even without the T.V., Neomi kind of liked his being gone cause she didn't have to go to church all the time. "I don't know what religion I am," she said, "but I know it ain't Baptist."

Bill was back before long, but things didn't get no better. One time we was fighting and he grabbed me by the thumb and pushed it back 'til it hurt. I tried to pull away but he held on tight. I weren't nowhere near as big as him, but I drug him through the whole house using my free hand to pick up anything I could hit him with. When we got to the kitchen, I picked up a glass bottle of R.C. Cola and tried to hit him with that. I missed and hit the kitchen counter with the bottle. He was laughing until then, but he didn't think it was so funny when I cut him two new eye brows with that broken R.C. bottle. He turned loose of my thumb and ran for a towel to wipe the blood off. I heard him dialing the telephone, no doubt calling Sheriff Womack.

"You gotta send somebody out here. My wife's gone crazy."

"Send them on out" I yelled, "I'll cut them, too."

I guess they heard me and reckoned I meant it, cause they didn't show up. After that, with them scars as a reminder of how rough it could get, we settled down a little bit, but things got bad again when I found out I was pregnant.

"I know we didn't plan on this, Bill, but I'm gonna have a baby."

"Now, I told you, Hazel, I got enough young'uns. I don't want no more. Yore just gonna have to get shed of it."

"You know I ain't gonna do that, Bill. I'm having this baby."

"Well, I don't want it, and I ain't gonna pay no doctor's bills nor childcare. Yore on yore own if you have it."

"You son of a bitch, I don't need yore help. I'll get me a job and take care of it myself."

I went to work at a sweat shop, Decatur Garment Manufacturing, making Army overcoats. They was already cut out when they arrived at the plant from up north, but we had to sew the pieces together and send the finished coats back up there. It was hot summertime, and the wool material was itchy. The work was hard, and I was getting bigger and feeling awful bad, but I hung in there. When I was six month along, I went to the hospital for a checkup. I was 36 years old and hadn't never had no pap smear, so I didn't suspect what they found. I had cancer in the womb.

The doctor said, "I shore am sorry to have to tell you this, Miz Hazel, but your cancer is too far advanced to let this baby go full term. If we don't take it, you're gonna die."

I shore didn't want to lose that baby, but I don't think they even give me a choice. It was a boy, and he only lived for just two hours. I named him David Emanuel. I was so sick I couldn't go to the funeral. That made me real sad, especially when I found out Bill didn't go, neither. Somebody took David's picture in his little casket and give it to me. I cried every time I looked at it.

Neomi, who was about 12 years old, went to the funeral, which was held at the Walnut Grove Cemetery, with my momma and my sister Geraldine. She said my daddy was there and he come up to her and asked, "Do you know who I am?"

Neomi shook her head. He said, "I'm yore granddaddy. I'm yore momma's daddy."

Neomi shook her head again. "Nuh uh," she said. "Yore too little to be my Grandpaw Lamb. He has to be a big man cause he used to beat up my Granny."

I don't know what my daddy said to that. He probably tucked his tail and tried to skulk off, hoping nobody heard her.

I was really suffering both in body and heart. The doctor said with radiation I might have two years to live. Bill wouldn't drive me to Chattanooga for the treatments. My momma didn't drive, but she would get one of my uncles to drive us.

In those days they treated cancer in the womb by putting cobalt inside. It made me awful sick and weak. The treatments, the travel, and the grief over my dead baby were all real hard on me. I couldn't hardly hold my head up. I spent most of the time in bed. One day when I was laying there, Bill come in and started choking me.

"You good for nothing bitch, laying there in the bed all the time. I told you to get rid of that baby. You might not be in this shape if you had listened to me."

I was too weak to fight back, but with my last breath I prayed. "Dear God, don't let me die. It'll break my momma's heart."

After he finished choking me and seen I was dead, he closed up the house real dark. He boarded up the windows, locked the doors, and just left me there. The next day when my momma come to check on me she couldn't get in.

"Fireball, you in there? Open up the door, baby. It's time to go to Chattanooga for yore treatment."

She had to knock out a window to get inside. She said she found me dead, but she washed my face and prayed over me'til I come back to life. When I begin to stir it made her so happy. She held me in her arms and let her tears pour over me, but I was too weak to know what was happening.

As soon as I was strong enough, Mommy got me to the doctor. When he saw the black and green marks on my neck he was shocked.

"Miz Hazel," the doctor asked, "what in hell happened to you?"

"My husband choked me to death."

He was astonished. "What did you marry?"

"A Sunday School superintendent," was my reply.

The doctor put me in a neck brace and said I would need to keep getting radiation treatments, but I told him Bill had took all my money and I was too sick to work. I didn't have no insurance.

"Well," he said, "if he lives, this is one bill that sorry S.O.B is going to pay."

The doctor went after him. He found out where he worked and got the money from his pay. That left Bill without enough money for a car or a place to live. He weren't very happy about it, but I thought he deserved his misery. People may wonder why he didn't go to prison for attempted murder, but we never called the law. That's not how our kind of people done things, even though I'd been married to a deputy sheriff.

After I had divorced Wilkerson and survived the cancer I went back to work at the coat factory. Two of my sisters was working there, too. The supervisor called us Tom, Dick, and Hazel.

One day I saw Bill on the street, and I told him, "You bastard, I'll know when you die."

"Aw, yore crazy. You aint gonna know nothing," he sneered.

He acted like he didn't believe me. But another time I seen him coming out of the grocery store when I was going in. When I come back out he was setting in my car.

"Son-of-a..., what the hell are you doing in my car?"

"Just go on and kill me now, Hazel."

"I may kill you now, or I may kill you 20 years from now. But get yore sorry ass outta my car this minute."

Eight years later when another husband and me was going fishing near Crossville Mountain we was listening on the car radio to a broadcast out of Meigs County.

"And now for the local news. Bill Wilkerson died in Decatur today."

"Thank you, God," was all I had to say.

CHAPTER 13:
BETWEEN WILKERSON AND TRUEBLOOD

I sold my house I'd lived in with the Colonel and Bill Wilkerson to my brother Lester and moved into a nearby mobile home. Neomi couldn't believe I was moving out of a good house into a trailer. But I guess there was too many bad memories there. I give $500 of the down payment Lester paid me to Neomi. She was a teenager at the time, so she was surprised I give her so much money. She said, "What do you want me to do with this money, Momma?"

She probably thought I wanted her to save it or buy school clothes, or something practical like that. But I said, "I don't care what you do with it, Neomi. Buy a baby elephant if you want to." Like I told the Colonel, it takes all the fun out of it when somebody gives you something and then they tell you what to do with it.

Now that Neomi was old enough, I set about teaching her how to drive. Much as she wanted to learn, she was embarrassed at the same time to be seen in my ugly old Chevy. She hoped she wouldn't meet nobody who'd recognize her. For me, it brought back memories of Uncle Hal teaching me to drive that Model T Ford when I was a young'un.

Neomi was a good driver and a good kid, so I didn't worry about her when she went back to Oak Ridge when school started up. She weren't wild and boy crazy like some girls was. She was determined to finish high school, and I was real proud of her.

Neomi and the Chevy

Although her daddy had remarried, I was okay with their living in the house 'til Neomi turned eighteen. Then the house and some of the land would be hers. I would give a few acres each to Butch and Dallas, but I didn't know if either of them would move back to Oak Ridge.

Dallas had married a girl named Edna in Columbus and they had a son, Tony. They wasn't married very long. Later he married Clara Bass in Decatur. They had two girls, Tanyia and Amanda. Butch married Evelyn Farmer in Decatur and they had a little girl they named Sherry after his sister that died the day he was born. That marriage was his only one. It didn't last very long neither.

I started dating a guy named Sandy. He was hot-headed, but his temper weren't no match for mine. Sandy called me a bitch one time, and I got my rifle out to shoot him. He jumped in a ditch, and ever time he raised his head I'd pull the trigger. He was wearing a red hat, which weren't too smart, cause I could see him real easy. I aimed just over his head, though. If I had meant to kill him, I would have. I never did drink no alcohol, and it's a good thing. With a temper like mine, I'd have gone to jail for sure if I had lost complete control of it.

I'll have to say this for Sandy, he didn't give up easy. When I ran out of bullets, he started coming closer. I had a carton of sixteen ounce Royal Crown Cola bottles inside the back door, so I told Neomi to hand

*Hazel with daughters-in-law
Evelyn and Edna. Butch holding
daughter Sherry in background.*

*Dallas with first wife, Edna, and
their son, Tony*

me one. I hit him with it so hard I dropped it. I told Neomi to hand me another one, and I hit him with that one, too. He was trying to dodge behind the corn crib, but I kept asking for R.C. bottles, Neomi kept handing them to me, and I kept hitting him. When we was out of empties, she held out a full bottle. "Momma," she said, "this one's got R.C. in it."

"Just give it to me, Neomi. I'll buy you another damned R.C," I answered impatiently.

Neomi weren't worried about losing her drink. She was just afraid I'd kill him if I hit him with a full bottle. She was nervous enough about what them empties could do if I hit him in the head with one. She didn't want me going to jail.

Sandy didn't take too well to my shooting at him and hitting him with R.C. bottles. Later he set fire to my momma's house and burned it down. But the next man I was to marry took care of Sandy, and he didn't bother me no more after that. And Neomi, to this day, hates R.C. Colas. But she still rags me saying, "I'll buy you another damned R.C., Neomi."

In all the times I got a drivers' license, business license, or marriage license, nobody ever asked to see my birth certificate. It's a good thing, cause I didn't have one. But in 1973, for some reason or another I had to have one. I was getting ready to deed some land to my children, so maybe that's why I had to have it. I went to the Meigs County Court House in Decatur and told the lady there what I wanted. She said she'd go find it and be right back. She was gone for what seemed like a long time just to make a copy of a birth certificate. But after a while she come back a shaking her head.

"I'm sorry, M'am, but we ain't got no birth record for a Hazel Neomi Lamb."

"Well," I said, "there's got to be one, cause here I am."

"Could it be under some other name?" she asked.

"I don't see how. It's the only name I've ever went by."

"Well, just hold on a minute. Let's see if I've got it right. That's January third, nineteen and thirty-one, right?"

I nodded.

"And your parents were Samuel Scott Lamb and Tilda Jane Lamb?"

"Uh huh," I nodded again.

"And you are sure you were born in Meigs County, Tennessee?"

"Couldn't a been nowhere else."

She sighed and shook her head. "Let me try again. You might want to set down on that bench over there. This could take a while to figure out."

I set down and waited. This time it weren't long before she come back.

"Are you sure your name ain't Rachael?"

"Rachael? Why in the world would my name be Rachael?"

"I don't know, M'am. But we have a birth record for a Rachel Lamb born to Samuel Scott Lamb and Tilda Howard Lamb on January third, nineteen thirty-one. Were you a twin?"

"Not that I ever knowed of."

"Well I think this has to be yores. And since you have been going by Hazel Neomi all these years, I think it would be best for us to change your name officially. I can do it now if you don't mind waiting just a little longer."

So I set down on that bench again and waited for her to finish so I could sign my name and legally be who I always thought I was.

When they finally sent me the altered birth certificate I found some other interesting details. From the way it was wrote, it looked like I was born on January 0, 1901 instead of January 3, 1931. I think I'm doing pretty good for a hundred and thirteen year old! I'm gonna keep celebrating my birthday on January third since it's hard to celebrate on a zero. And I ain't gonna claim to be older than my momma, who was born in 1910, no matter what my birth certificate says.

CHAPTER 14:
JAMES TRUEBLOOD

James Trueblood

You'd think I would of swore off of men after the Sunday School super-intendent turned out so bad and Sandy was such a nuisance. And I did have the longest break I'd had between husbands. But I had not met the sweetest one yet.

I had gone to work at a furniture manufacturing place and my job was upholstering. I was managing a crew when a young, good-looking guy named James Trueblood come to work there. He was a nice feller, and we hit it off real good. We both loved music. In fact, playing guitars and singing was what really brought us together. I was a lot older than him, and I was trying to match him up with a girl his age. Lots of girls wanted to date him.

"James," I said, "you seen that pretty little blond headed gal that just come to work here? She wants to go out with you."

"I don't think so."

"You ought to go in there and talk to her. She seems real sweet."

"I ain't interested."

I was busy rebuilding my momma's house after Sandy burned it down, and James offered to help me with it. He was a hard worker, and we managed real good together. I liked him and kept trying to fix him up with another girl, but he always said, "Not interested."

I told him he needed to find a good woman and settle down. Finally he said, "Hazel, if I can't have you, I don't want nobody."

I didn't hardly know what to say to that. I had no idea he was interested in me that-a-way. "Why, James," I said, "What would yore family think about that?"

"Don't really care what nobody thinks."

"But what are you gonna say when people laugh at you for being with a woman nearly twice your age? I'm old enough to be yore momma.

"You are old enough to be my wife, and I would be real proud to have you. I'll get down on my knees if you want me to."

"Now, James, be sensible."

"If I don't marry you, Hazel, I'll die single."

That's when I realized James was crazy about me. He promised he'd be good to me, and he said he'd never look at another woman. "I'm like a hair in a biscuit, Hazel. I'm here to stay."

I believed him. He was so sweet and so good, he just won me over. We both had mean daddies and sweet mommas, and we had the same ideas about how folks ought to live. We would have been like brother and sister if we hadn't fallen in love. He said the day we got married was the best day of his life.

Hazel and James on their wedding day

James was plenty smart, but he never went to school, and he hadn't learnt to write. So I taught him. We practiced writing the names of the states and all kinds of other stuff. But he was proudest when he finally could write these words: Hazel I love you.

Hazel and James in their antique store

Me and James opened an antique shop in Decatur, and it was going real good. I was happier than I'd ever been before. But then we found out James had cancer. At first he didn't tell me his balls was hurting real bad, but then they swole up so big it weren't no secret no more.

I took him to a clinic in Athens, but the doctor there acted like there weren't nothing bad wrong. He even said James was just feeling sorry for hisself. So I took him to a good doctor I knowed about in Oak Ridge. He said James had testicular cancer and if we hadn't came when we did, he would of died.

Ever time I got a bill from that doctor in Athens, it made me real mad, so I wrote a check for twenty-five cents and mailed it to him. They couldn't say I weren't making payments. After a little while they stopped sending bills. I guess they seen it was costing them more for mailing than what they was getting from me. I didn't mind paying the doctor in Oak Ridge who was trying his best to help us.

James took radiation and was able to stay home for a while, but he started getting bad again. We went back to the hospital, but they wasn't able to stop the cancer. While he was dying my heart was breaking. I wrote him this poem and read it to him in the hospital two days before he died:

My Chest Freezer

My chest is a freezer built to preserve my heart.
To keep fresh the love we knew right from the start.
To keep all our sweet memories after we are apart.
No it's not that you are leaving me for someone new.
It's just that God has other plans for you.

I recall all the thrills. The short beats of my heart.
On that glad day we joined hands before the man
As he said until death do you part.
Now I feel the pain. The teardrops as they start.
For I hear Jesus whisper. Now death do you part.

Now I'll take all my blessings, and the good times we knew
And lock them in my chest freezer.
Along with all the sweet memories of you.
You hold my hand and kiss it and ask me not to cry.
But Honey I can't help it. For you see I'm watching you die.

Good-Bye now darling. It really hurts to see you go.
But God only chooses the best. So I guess that's why you have to go.
So I'll keep our love locked in my chest freezer and work hard here
below.
And maybe it won't be long until I'm good enough to go.

(Note: Some spelling corrections made for clarity.)

James was just 28 years old when he died on May 12, 1973. We buried him in the Walnut Grove Cemetery. When he died he had 10 pictures of me in his billfold. If he had lived, I think he would of been my last husband.

CHAPTER 15:
E.V. WATSON

Not long after I buried James, Neomi got married to a boy named Alan Watson, and they moved down to Douglasville, Georgia. She had met him the day she turned sixteen and married him at eighteen. Unlike her momma, she'd finished high school and hadn't dated a lot of different guys. She'd spent summers with me ever since I divorced her daddy, and I'm shore she didn't want to move from place to place with different husbands like I done. She wanted one marriage to last a lifetime, and we was both hopeful this would work out for her.

Neomi and Hazel

I was still heart broke over losing James. I didn't know what to do with myself. So I decided to move to Georgia to be near Neomi. Down there I met Alan's uncle E.V. Watson, who was like a daddy to Alan. In fact, he had practically raised him since he was a teenager. Alan's daddy was military, and since they moved a lot he didn't bother making him go to school much. Allen and E.V. worked together as carpenters, and ever since Alan was old enough to get his driver's license E.V. had been depending on him to drive him around when he was drinking.

I later learnt that E.V. had been rough on Alan, trying to teach him to be tough. Alan said one time he was setting in a car with his uncle, and he told him, "Boy, don't never let nobody do this to you." And E.V. got out of the car, walked around to the passenger side where Alan was setting, opened the door, leaned in, and punched him hard in the face with his fist. Course, we didn't know none of this at the time, so we had no reason to think Alan had been abused or wouldn't be good to Neomi.

Before I could turn around good, I was getting married to E.V. We moved into an apartment not far from Neomi and Alan. But it seems E.V. weren't through dealing with his ex-wife, who lived in Anderson County, Tennessee. I come home one day and found a note saying, "Gone streaking to Tennessee." It was kind of a fad back then to take off yore clothes and run through a place where people could see you. They called it "streaking." He was trying to make a little joke, but it weren't funny to me. I was shore he was headed up there to see his ex-wife, Georgie.

I moved out of that apartment and into one across the street. I took everything that was mine including the curtains. Neomi asked me weren't I gonna leave him something to cover the windows with, and I said, "Nope. If he's a streaking, he don't need no curtains."

And as it turned out, he didn't need no curtains. When he showed up at Georgie's house, she shot him right through the door. Killed him deader than a doornail. She claimed he used to beat her up when they was married and she was afraid he was there to do it again. If that was true, I didn't blame her one little bit for what she done. Some people believe it was her son, not her, who shot him. But nobody ever went to jail for it.

Neomi was scared she might come shoot me, too, but I never had no contact with her. If E.V. had told me he still wanted to be with her, I'd a give him the divorce papers to take with him. I never understood folks who wouldn't stop pestering their exes. When I mark one off, he's gone. After I leave him, I don't give a shit what he does or who with. Too bad E.V. weren't more like me.

When both me and Neomi was living in Georgia, it was the only time our place in Oak Ridge was ever rented out, and that was a big mistake. Amos was required to move out when Neomi turned eighteen. We had left my sister Geraldine responsible for the house, and she rented it to the meanest biker in Tennessee. He didn't take care of the place. He painted spider webs on the walls and left tracks on the floor from where he rode his motorcycle through the house. He made a big mess where he grew marijuana plants and dried them, and neighbors said he even run around outside naked!

Neomi and Alan

I decided it was time to take that place back, so I sent him packing and moved back to Oak Ridge. I got me a job waiting tables at Shoney's and pretty soon become the manager on the night shift. Neomi decided to move back, too, and she got on at Shoney's working the day shift. Her marriage to Alan was not going well, and though he moved into an apartment with her, he weren't home much. She was determined to make a go of it, so she put up with more than I would of.

Neomi got pregnant, but she lost the baby. Later she got pregnant again and gave birth to her son Jason on October 25, 1975. I was with Neomi for the birth, and Alan was there, too, but he left again and didn't see his son for three months.

It would of been better if Alan hadn't came back at all. Two nurses lived across the road from Neomi. One day one of them called me.

"Hazel," she said, "you better get down here. Yore son-in-law is dragging yore daughter by her hair face-down across the yard."

"I'm on my way," I shouted, throwing down the phone.

I grabbed my keys, jumped in my car, and drove as as fast as I could go. I got to Neomi's place in less than ten minutes. The nurse that had called me met me outside.

"You better not go in there, Hazel. He's already throwed out two big old men who tried to go help her."

"You telling me my daughter's in there and I ain't to go in? He may look like a wrestler to you, but he looks like Ned in the first reader to me."

I opened the door. "Momma, please don't come in here," Neomi begged.

I ignored her plea and went inside and found my daughter and grandson on the bed. Alan was setting on a chair and had Neomi by the arm. "You take yore filthy hand off my daughter," I said to him.

"Momma, go outside. He'll kill you."

"I got one way to go and one time to go, Neomi. I ain't afraid of dying."

I handed her my car keys and said, "Take that baby and go get in my car. If I'm not out in 15 minutes, call the police cause I'll be dead."

"Don't you take those keys, Neomi," Alan growled, letting go of her arm and standing up.

"Baby," I said to Neomi, "have I ever lied to you? All he does is lie. But I'm gonna take care of you and this baby. So take these keys and y'all get on out there right now."

She done like I said, and I turned to him. "If you ever lay a hand on her or that baby again, I will kill you, or I'll die trying."

He sat back down, not trying to stop me as I walked out the door. I took Neomi and Jason home with me. The next day I got a phone call from the nurse who had called me before.

"Could you come back out here?" she asked

I was shore Alan had come back and was tearing things up. "I'm on my way," I shouted once again. But when I got there, he was nowhere in sight. The nurse had a woman with her. She apologized for rushing me out there. "I told my neighbor here about this little bitty woman who come out here madder'n a bull and went in there and got her daughter after that man had already throwed out two big old men. She didn't believe me, cause she knowed yore son-in-law was big and strong as an ox."

I was relieved I didn't have to mess with him again, so I was okay about it, and even let them take my picture. But I did have to comment, "I didn't see nobody trying to take no pictures while I was dealing with that son of a bitch."

Neomi weren't ready to give up on her marriage, but now she was scared of Alan. He would threaten her by saying he'd do to her what Georgie done to E.V. if she tried to leave. So she stuck it out nearly five more years before she finally got the courage to go. She was letting me keep Jason most of the time, and on the morning of March 27, 1980, she left for work with just her purse and the clothes on her back, and she never went back there again. She remembered what she said when she was a kid about if she left a man she was gonna take everthing but his clothes she couldn't wear. That shore seemed like a foolish girl's promise now, after all of what she had went through. She left all her size zero pants with that two hundred pound man.

Most folks don't never change. My daddy didn't. He was the same son of a bitch when he was buried as he was when he was alive. But I seen Alan again nearly forty years later when him and his sister come to see Jason one day. Alan had lost a hundred pounds since I seen him last, and I didn't recognize him. We got to talking about when Jason was a little boy, and I said what a son of a bitch his daddy was. Alan's sister almost fell off her chair a laughing, cause she figured I must not of recognized him.

Alan weren't laughing. "Hazel," he said, "what you said is true. I can't deny it. But I have tried, over the years, to become a better man and be a good father to Jason. And I am sorry for how I treated Neomi. He went on to say how the death of his parents made him think about his own life. I reckon maybe he was one who really did change for the better.

CHAPTER 16:
BETWEEN WATSON AND DOWNS

About six months before Neomi left Alan she had started learning how to be a pipe fitter. Alan's Uncle Von, who had encouraged her to leave him, told her that pipe fitting was a job that paid good. He said it would provide insurance, too, which she and Jason would need. Neomi didn't even know what a pipefitter was, but she was twenty-five years old and smart, and Von was shore she would learn real fast.

Neomi was one of over two hundred people who applied for that year's apprenticeship with Rust Engineering that was located at the Oak Ridge K-25 plant. She was one of twenty-five that they accepted. She had to work as an apprentice forty hours a week and go to school in Knoxville for four hours two nights a week. I was able to watch Jason for her, which took a load off her mind.

Neomi didn't think nothing about doing men's work cause she seen me doing it all her life. She become the second woman apprentice in the Plumbers and Steamfitters's Local 102 in Knoxville. The other female apprentice dropped out, so Neomi was the only woman to finish in that class. I was so proud of her, and I knowed for shore she'd do real good.

When she was a teenager, Neomi would take her daddy to work at the plant, dropping him off at the guard gate in the morning and picking him up there in the afternoon. With armed guards at the gates and barbed wire on the top of the walls, to her it seemed like a prison. Amos told her a siren sounded to tell him when he could eat lunch and when he could go home. He said there was five different sirens that give off different warnings. One of them meant get in your car and get out fast. Amos told her she ought to get a job there, too, when she graduated from high school, cause she could make good money. But she had said she didn't want to. It was too scary. But she had a kid to think about, so a good income was what mattered now.

Neomi and Jason

Four generations

At some point Neomi needed her birth certificate, and that's when we found out her name was spelled Naomi, not Neomi. She had to use that for work, so from then on she started calling herself Naomi. But I never stopped calling her Neomi. Somebody asked her how come she didn't know how to spell it right, and she said, "When you learn how to spell yore name as a little kid, you don't ask to see yore birth certificate."

Jason was always right with me while his momma was at work. No matter what I was doing, he wanted to do it, too. He was dragging tools behind me before he was big enough to pick them up. He got real handy with a hammer and saw when he was just a little feller. He also helped me with the hogs. One day we was fixing to go slop them, and he looked up at me with a serious look on his face and said, "Mam Maw, if I work real hard, will you buy me a six pack of chocolate beers?"

That really tickled me, cause I knowed he was talking about Yoohoo chocolate drinks. But he'd seen folks drinking beer – which I didn't approve of – and he thought if it come in a bottle it was beer.

I had learnt upholstery work at the factory in Decatur where I met James. And I had did a lot of reupholstering when we had the antique shop there. I could take the old covering off and make a pattern for a new cover for any chair or sofa. Now I decided to go into business doing that kind of work in Oak Ridge. I found a suitable building on Warehouse Road, bought me some good sturdy equipment and a bunch of fabric, and before long I had a steady stream of customers.

I got a contract with the Oak Ridge Hospital to reupholster their wheel chairs when the fabric was wore through and the stuffing was a showing. One day I was there in my truck picking up some chairs when I seen an orderly pushing a woman out to the patient pick-up area. He had some papers under his arm, but they kept falling out. He'd have to stop, stoop down, and pick them up. He looked real frustrated, but he had to have both hands to push that wheel chair, so there weren't no way them papers was gonna stay under his arm. I got an idea about solving his problem. So when I brought them chairs back, each one had a nice deep pocket on the back, big enough to hold a bunch of papers. I was real proud of that invention, and the folks at the hospital liked it a lot, too.

Dallas and his second wife, Clara, and their two girls, Amanda and Taynia, was now living in Oak Ridge. Dallas had gone to work in the coal mines, and Clara helped me in the upholstery shop. Butch had stayed in Meigs County while I was in Georgia, but when I come back to Oak Ridge, he moved up there and worked with us, too. Butch and Clara was especially helpful with the lifting when I had a heavy chair or sofa to work on.

Jason was always there, as well, and was quick to learn ways to help out. But I had to keep an eye on him and some of his little buddies who liked to hang around. I had a cold drink machine, but I didn't seem to ever break even when I refilled it and emptied out the coins. One day I

Dallas and Clara

Clara and Hazel

heared Jason tell his friends, "You don't have to pay. I know where Mam Maw keeps the key."

I watched Jason take the key out of the cash register drawer, open the machine, and pass around Coca Colas and Nehi sodas. I appreciated him being generous, but I told him he was gonna break me if he kept that up, and that he was at least gonna have to ask me first before he treated his little friends.

My sister Geraldine was still living nearby, and me and her liked going to yard sales and flea markets ever Saturday morning. Pretty soon I was buying stuff and selling it at flea markets myself. I also made deals to clean out houses when somebody old died or moved into a rest home and their kids wanted to sell the house as fast as possible. I was surprised that folks didn't care nothing about the things their mommas and daddies had worked so hard for all their lives. All they could see was fast dollars when the house sold, so I got a lot of good things to sell.

One time I was cleaning out a house and I found a big box of school pictures, report cards, and pictures the kids had drew when they was little. I just knowed the folks who hired me was gonna be so excited when they seen it. It shore would of thrilled me if I'd found stuff like that from when I was little. But they acted like it was just trash and told me to get rid of it. I couldn't believe they didn't care about this part of their history. Didn't they want to show it to their kids? But they said, "Naw, we don't have no need for that old junk." I kept it for a long time. I just couldn't bring myself to disrespect their old folks, even though they wasn't my parents.

Jason would help me collect stuff, and he liked to go with me and his Aunt Gerley to the flea market where I had started selling it. Sometimes we would leave him at our booth and go looking around. We was always surprised when we come back at how much he sold. He was a charmer, and I guess people liked this little old boy who was helping his granny make a living.

Sometimes I run across little trinkets I liked that I'd keep for myself. I had a skull and crossbones on a chain I dangled from my rear view mirror in my truck. Then I found a pretty little leaf that I hung up there with it. Somebody asked me why I had that marijuana leaf hanging there with that skeleton. I said one was to show you what you'd look life if you smoked the other one.

I met all kinds of people at the flea market, and I never knowed what kind of crazy questions they'd ask me. Most of them just wanted to know if you had some hard-to-find item they was looking for or if I'd take a ridiculous low price for something they had a hankering for, but one woman really took the cake. She told me she was looking for somebody to kill her.

I thought that woman was joking at first, but she kept saying she wanted somebody to take a gun and shoot her. I said, "You want somebody else to go to the pen for killing you? If that's what you want, put a gun under yore chin and shoot yore own self." She walked off, but I watched her stop at ever booth she come to, and folks just shook their heads. I think she was a few spots short of something.

Sometimes Neomi would go with me to antique stores and junk shops to find things to keep or resell. One time we was at a store and I found some old fishing equipment that was in good shape. It had a price on it I thought was reasonable, so I counted out the money and told the woman who owned the shop I'd like to buy it. It turned out them things had belonged to her husband that had died. As I started to hand her the money, she began a wailing and saying. "Oh, my pore old John. He was a policeman, and his greatest joy in life was fishing. It breaks my heart to let his collection go."

I felt real sorry for her. I thought about how much my momma loved to fish and how much I missed her. "You don't have to sell them right now," I said, pulling the money back.

"Oh," she said, reaching for the cash, "I never liked that old son of a bitch, anyhow."

I couldn't help but laugh.

Neomi found some things she wanted to buy from this same woman. She asked Neomi, "Would you be willing to pay for them now but not get them until I die?"

Neomi didn't go for that idea and said, "No, M'am."

I still liked to sing and dance and play my guitar, and one of my favorite places to go was the Ciderville Music Barn out on the Clinton Highway. It was kind of famous, cause Cas Walker, who we used to watch when the kids was little, done his popular T.V. show from there now. A lot of famous country singers like Dolly Parton got their start on the Cas Walker Farm and Home Show when it was on the radio. Now people come from far and near to hear David West, the owner, on the banjo with all the other musicians and singers. I met some famous people who was performing there, and I guess meeting Kitty Wells, who was about seventy or eighty years old, was one of the highlights of my life. Me and Mommy had listened to her or the first radio we ever got. She was real sweet.

Ciderville was, and still is, a country jubilee place where they didn't serve no alcohol, so lots of little kids would be there. Some of their mommas and daddys would drop them off cause they knowed it was a safe place, and they'd go on to a honky tonk where they could get liquor.

And some of them little kids come with mommas who just wanted to find a cowboy to snuggle up with on the dance floor. I seen them setting there with their sad little faces watching people dance. I could tell they really wanted to do it, too. So I'd go over to them and coax them out on the floor. They was shy at first, but I'd tap my shoes that clicked and jingled and in no time a tall I'd have them dancing and a grinning. It would tickle me when I'd hear them hollering, "Miz Hazel, Miz Hazel," wanting me to dance with them. I bought tap shoes for some of them young'uns, and they'd get so excited learning to buck dance in them.

At first I was scared their mommas might not want me taking them out on the dance floor like that, but some of them come up after and thanked me, especially the ones that found a man without them kids hanging on them.

I'd be out on the floor a dancing, and then I'd get interrupted by David West. He'd holler out, "We're gonna do a special song for Squatting Heifer."

And I'd call back, "Atta boy, Setting Bull." Then they'd play one of my favorites like "It Wasn't God Who Made Honky Tonk Angels" or "Yore Cheatin Heart."

And then he'd say, "You ready to come sing for us, Squatting Heifer?" We kidded each other with those names so much, we almost didn't know who folks was talking about when they called us by our real names. One of my boyfriends complained, "You sorry dog, that's an awful name to put on a pretty women." But I didn't mind. In fact I was the one who come up with it. He was a bull and I was a heifer. He was setting and I was squatting. I didn't see no difference. When I met David we went together like two buzzards. We was like brother and sister, and he was always real good to me. We was always cutting up one way or the other. One time he even let me put taps on his shiny black patent leather shoes.

I loved singing and joking around with the folks who come to Ciderville. I was there ever Saturday night for both shows. Me and David called it "The Roaring Eighties," and I was having the time of my life. I still had to get up and work the next day, so I didn't sleep much. As

Setting Bull put it, "We don't get much rest, and there's two reasons for it – we work too hard and we're afraid we'll miss something if we don't show up." Even after he got rich as ten foot up a bull, David stayed simple as a foot log.

A woman who was one of the regulars there was complaining one night about unfaithful men. "Hazel," she asked, "why do you think men feel like they need an extra woman?"

"I guess they think they need a spare in case they have a flat," was my reply.

One of my favorite performers at Ciderville was an old woman named Hattie. Hattie must have been at least eighty-five years old. She worked with a partner, a young fella named Silas. One joke they liked to do went like this.

Silas would ask, "How many times you been married, Hattie?"

"Three times," she answered proudly.

"What happened to your first husband?"

"He died."

"He died? How did he die?"

"He ate some poison mushrooms."

"Poison mushrooms? That's terrible. What happened to your second husband?"

"He died."

"And how did he die, Hattie?"

"He ate some poison mushrooms."

"Well, what about your third husband. Is he still alive?"

"No, he's dead."

"Poison mushroom?" Silas asked, nodding his head up and down, like he knowed the answer.

"No, he died from a slash wound across his fore head."

"My goodness. How did that happen?"

"He wouldn't eat his mushrooms."

That always got a big laugh, no matter how many times they done that routine. And most folks didn't realize Silas was really Hattie's son. It wouldn't of been near as funny if they knowed that.

Silas and Hattie

Jason liked to go to Ciderville with me cause they had cake walks during intermission. He loved walking around on the numbers and stopping still when the music quit playing. He was always hoping he'd win a cake, and lots of times he did. I think he got more enjoyment out of the cake walking and winning than he did out of eating the cake, and he liked cake a lot.

When David found out I had opened my upholstery shop, he asked if I'd be interested in redoing the seats in a 1937 Pontiac he was restoring. I said I reckon I could even though I never had done no automobile upholstery before. The car was green, so I done the seat covers in green and black, and they turned out real nice. People told David them seats shore did set good. They said they looked and felt like a studio couch. Some folks wanted to know who done it, and he would brag on me, saying I was a hard worker and self-taught. I appreciated his high regard, and it brought me some more good customers.

I danced a lot with little kids, but I also had plenty of grown up dance partners at Ciderville. One of them was the Anderson County road supervisor. He thought I was "it," and he would patiently wait his turn to dance with me. But another man was my favorite partner, and it wouldn't be long before he'd be husband number nine.

CHAPTER 17:
FLOYD DOWNS, JR., AND JOHN BRYAN

A man named Floyd Downs, Jr., lived just up the hill from Ciderville, and I seen him there all the time. He was balding but good looking. Jason liked teasing him about his bald spot. Of course Jason tormented all my boyfriends.

Floyd was kind of short like me and a good dancer. He was a pretty good song writer, too. We sung some of his songs together. And he smiled so much some people wondered about him, but I just laughed and said, "He ain't crazy, but he carries a light load."

I think Floyd may have already heard I had a reputation with guns, but one day he asked me, "Hazel, can you shoot a pistol?"

"Yep," I replied.

"Do you have a gun?" he asked.

"About five of them, I reckon. You want to go do some shooting?"

We walked up the hill to his house, and he put up a target on a tree in the back yard. I told him to go first. Well, he shot about eight or ten times, all around that target. Then I took the gun and on the first shot I hit the center and knocked the target down. He didn't say nothing, but I could tell by the look on his face he didn't like it that I was a better shot than him. That didn't make him lose interest, though.

It seemed like ever guy I ever dated wanted to marry me. When Floyd asked me, I said, "You just think you want to be married to me, but I don't put up with much. You need to be bullet proof."

But I married him next, number nine.

Floyd was a sign painter. I made room for him to have a shop in my upholstery place. His regular job was at Union Carbide where he worked with Neomi. He painted her name on the hard hat she had to wear for protection on the job.

I don't remember Floyd ever talking about knowing Buford Pusser, the "Walking Tall" sheriff, but I found this picture of the two of them. Pusser was from Tennessee, so maybe they did know each other.

Floyd and Hazel Downs

On the back somebody wrote:
Buford (Walking Tall) Pusser
Junior (Walking Short) Downs

My marriage to Floyd must have been a pretty good one. It lasted 3 years. Neomi says he loved me unconditionally, but I kind of treated him like a little kid. He was easy going and quiet, but he was quick to brag on what a hard worker I was, saying I worked like a man. Neomi said the reason I couldn't stay with a man was because they couldn't keep up with me and I wore them all out. I don't remember no bad details with Floyd, but with me, when it's done, it's done. I don't see no need in spending time looking back.

When we split up, I told Junior he had to get the divorce, although it was clear he didn't want me to quit him. I guess I had two husbands for a little bit, cause I got married again faster than he got around to filing those papers. When I commenced to wondering about it, I went to see Floyd. He said, "Hazel, I just couldn't bring myself to divorce you."

"Well," I said, "I know you are as slow as steam off cold water, but you gotta do it quick cause I don't want to go to jail." So he put a rush on it, and I didn't have to do no time.

Hazel and John Bryan on wedding day

Sometimes it seemed like I was playing hop scotch. I'd hop off one husband and on to another one. Somebody said I went through husbands like Sherman went through Georgia. John Bryan was next. He worked at a plant in Oak Ridge. I divorced this one cause he called me a bitch. He got down on his knees and begged me to stay. But I said, "You don't call me a bitch and still sleep with me." He even sent some of his friends to ask me would I take him back. But he'd had his chance. I'd already moved on.

I was still raising hogs, and at one point I had 160 of them. I sold a lot of them to Wamper's Farm Sausage Company. Local people bought a lot of my pork, too. Neomi had got on at Martin Marietta, and she would get orders from folks she worked with there.

One day a young feller named Dave Davenport come by my place with a load of wood he wanted to swap for a ham. I could always use extra wood in the smoke house, so he had a deal. He was also interested in buying some land around there. I didn't know it then, but in time, he would become my son-in-law. I weren't too crazy about him at first, but he growed on me.

We always butchered our own hogs, but we did have to have some help. One of our neighbors, Luther Stooksbury, helped us a lot, and Gerald Forsyth would come down when we needed to neuter the hogs we planned to butcher. Only a male hog that we wanted to use as a sire to produce new piglets got to keep all his parts.

One time Gerald had to give mouth-to-mouth to a hog he held too tight when they was getting ready to neuter him. The pig stopped breathing, so Gerald got down on his knees, put his mouth over that hog's mouth, and blew into it with all he was worth. The pig lived, but Luther and folks he told about it never quit ragging Gerald about giving CPR to a pig. They already kidded him a lot about his well-known love of mountain oysters, so this was just one more thing pore old Gerald had to tolerate.

When it come to hogs, I would do everthing but kill them. I slopped them when they was living, and I dressed them out when they was dead. But I just couldn't bring myself to shoot them. When I was little, even though I learnt to shoot a gun early, I didn't like to go hunting. I didn't have no stomach for killing nothing. But when my uncles would bring us a mess of squirrels they had shot, after they was dead I didn't mind skinning and gutting them. But I seen my daddy torture helpless animals, and I guess that's why I just couldn't bear it.

One time there was this biker guy visiting at hog-killing time, and he bragged he was a real good shot. He wanted to know if he could shoot one, and I said okay. But he shot that sow four or five times and she didn't fall over. It made me mad he was letting her suffer. I grabbed the rifle out of his hands and shot that pig between the eyes and put her out of her misery. I felt like shooting that son of a bitch.

The biggest pig I ever raised was a Yorkshire that Jason named Colombo. He was judged the largest hog in Anderson County, weighing in at over 1100 pounds. Jason and Dallas's girl Amanda would ride him like a pony. I used him as a sire, so when he outlived his usefulness, I donated him to the Museum of Appalachia in Clinton. When Jason was ten years old his class went on a field trip there and he said he seen him. I bet he really bragged to his classmates that his Mam Maw raised that pig. I don't think it ever bothered him that his grandmaw weren't like most kids' grannies.

Dave and Colombo

I had a bunch of different boyfriends after I divorced Bryan. One was a boy Dave knowed named Barry Stewart. I met him when I was playing guitar at a picnic. He had a pretty head of long dark hair and a dark beard. He was real good looking. I was in my fifties, and he was about twenty-five. He was younger than Neomi, who liked him a lot and joked if I married him, she'd call him "Daddy." Neomi didn't usually joke like that, cause it would always make her mad when somebody would ask, "How many daddies have you got?"

She always replied, "I ain't got but one daddy. How many you got?"

Hazel and Barry

When I met Barry he was living in a teepee in Oliver Springs. He was real handy and helped me put up some of the buildings around my house. He also helped me with the pigs. One time we was slopping the hogs and one got a bone caught in its throat. Barry hollered at me, "Hazel, this pigs choking. What do I do?"

"Cut its throat!" I yelled back.

Later he said, "Hazel, I hope I don't never get choked around you."

Another time Butch walked by where me and Barry was laying in the grass just dying laughing. Barry smoked pot, which I never did. But Butch thought we must both be high, as hard as we was laughing.

When I was able to stop laughing and catch my breath long enough, I told Butch that Colombo, who we hadn't got shed of yet, was trying to mount a sow and she backed him and his big old mountain oysters into the electric fence. "You ain't seen nothing," I said, "til you see a thousand pound hog flying through the air."

Sometimes Barry would go with me to Edward's Steakhouse to get their left over scraps for the hogs. There was a woman there who was always remarking on how young he was. One time she asked another woman, "Have you seen her young, good looking boyfriend?"

I couldn't resist saying, "He asked me to marry him on my fiftieth birthday. And I may just have to, cause I think I'm pregnant!"

Barry was a good guy, but we moved on. I heard he later become a doctor, and I was real proud for him. I also learnt that he got married and him and his wife had two children. He give them kids the same names as my grandchildren, Jason and Amanda. I think they was the only little young'uns he'd ever been around.

I decided to move my upholstery business back to my house to save money. I had enough satisfied customers to stay busy, so I didn't need to have no place for walk-ins. Word had got around to all kinds of people who needed my services. I even reupholstered the motorcycle seat for the president of the Outlaws Motorcycle Club.

I thought it was kind of odd that I didn't make no clothes for my kids to wear when they was growing up. I had wore outfits my momma made us from flour and feed sacks, and I guess I wanted my kids to have better, so I bought them ready-made clothes. I weren't no seamstress, but I was real good at covering furniture.

For a while I worked out of my house, but it really crowded me and made a constant mess. So I bought a building from an old saw mill and moved the 10 foot by 10 foot sections one piece at a time to build a separate building behind my house for the upholstery work.

I had an accident with a skill saw while I was working on that building. I had finished cutting a board and went to set the saw down. The guard didn't close like it was supposed to, and I wound up cutting a gash in my leg right above the knee. My boyfriend, a seventy years old man named Robert, tooked me to the doctor, and I had to have it stitched up. Me and Robert didn't date long. He died of heat stroke.

* * *

Nineteen eighty-four started out hard. Mommy died of cancer on my birthday, January 3. I was sad, but I knowed, good as she was, there weren't no chance of her missing heaven. I always believed she'd outlive my daddy, but he was still alive.

In November of the next year I lost Butch. He was living with me, working with me, and we was playing music together. We was real close. It seemed like half of my life was took away from me when he died.

Butch had been complaining of a stomach ache and vomiting for about three days. That night he was sleeping on the couch. Jason was sleeping on the floor by him. They was real close, too. Butch had always took up a lot of time with Jason, all the time taking him to ball games and such.

During the night Butch woke Jason up and said for him to wake me up. He said he was needing to go to the hospital. I told Jason to go get his momma and daddy to help me put him in my car. They come real fast and we tried to set him up in the back seat of my Chevy, but he said he couldn't set up. So me and Dave and Neomi got in the front seat, and Butch laid all scrunched up on the back seat. Jason was wedged in on the floor between the front and back seats.

When we got to the hospital Butch told us not to let them make him set up, so Neomi told the emergency room orderly that come out to meet us with a wheelchair to go get a stretcher. But he said if he could come to the hospital in a car, he could ride in a wheelchair. We was protesting, and Butch was groaning real bad, but that orderly told us to stay in the waiting room, and he wheeled him down the hall. I tried to follow him, but Neomi held me back and said we had to wait there. It weren't long at all before a nurse come out and told us Butch was dead.

I wanted to know what caused it, but they wasn't sure. They didn't do no autopsy or nothing like that, but later we found out his daddy, Amos, had trouble with his pancreas and eventually Neomi would, too, so maybe that was what caused him to die. It just broke my heart to lose another child, even though he weren't little like the other two I lost. Yore children is supposed to outlive you, not the other way around.

Chapter 18:
Bill Lindsey

Bill and Hazel

I was still meeting most of my boyfriends at country jubilees. There was several besides Ciderville I liked going to in Anderson County. One was held on Saturday nights at the Norris Community Center off Highway 441. Another was the Chapman Highway Jubilee, and one of my favorites, and the one where I was to meet my next husband, was a place called The Picking Parlor in Oak Ridge. It was in an old barn near Anderson County High School.

I told Neomi I was dating another guy named Bill. (I must of liked the name Bill, cause I dated and married quite a few of them.)

"What's his last name, Momma?" she asked.

"I don't know, Neomi. I ain't asked him that."

"You don't know his last name and yore a dating him?"

"Last names don't matter unless you got kids going to school," I replied.

Well that weren't enough for Neomi. I wouldn't of let her date nobody whose last name she didn't know, and I guess she felt the same way about who I dated. So her and Dave and Jason decided to come to the jubilee and check him out.

When they got there they seen me getting out of his truck. He was a square dancer, and he had a bumper sticker that said, "Do-si-do" on it. Dave misread it and asked, "What's a doo-sie-doo?" That tickled Neomi, and she explained it was a square dance step. When Neomi spotted Bill, she realized he was Bill Lindsey. She knowed him cause they both had worked at Martin Marietta, so she said it was okay for me to date him.

By this time Neomi and Dave was married. They had had a big outdoor wedding at our place. It was attended by a strange mix of people. Dave invited all his biker friends. Some of them come from as far away as Detroit. And then there was a bunch of scientists who worked with Neomi who come, too. But they all got along just fine and everbody had a real good time.

Neomi and Dave

All-in-all, Dave's been good to Neomi and Jason. Somebody asked me how I could be shore he was a good one. I said cause I had used up all the bad ones. I worried, though, about Neomi and Dave because they liked to go drinking at bars. They'd leave on his motor bike, but they'd call me to come get them when they was ready to come home. On our way home we would pass a cemetery that was all lit up. One night Neomi remarked, "That's where I want to be buried when I die."

We had talked about having a family burial plot on our land, so I asked her why she wanted to be buried in that cemetery. She said, "Cause they leave the lights on at night."

I said, "Neomi, I think you are drunker that you realize."

After we dated a little while, Bill and me decided to get married at the jubilee where we met. We had a woman preacher marry us. Her name was Mrs. Ida Mae Dalton. I don't recall too much about how she looked, but I do remember she was wearing the brightest pink lipstick I ever seen.

Bill was retired from Martin Marietta and owned a home in Kingston, but I never went there. He also had a place on the lake at the Tri-County Sportsman's Club, and we stayed there a lot. It had two bedrooms and a nice sun porch we liked to set on when we wasn't out fishing for blue gill and crappie. I thought about my momma a lot and how much she loved to fish. I missed her more than ever when I was at the lake. But Jason, who was about fourteen years old, and a friend of his named Casey helped us remodel the lake house, so they was there a lot, which I liked.

The house next door was real close to Bill's, and a nudist lived there. I told that feller he better not come in our yard without no clothes on. I said if I seen him naked I was a real good shot and I'd shoot that thing off.

I still had my place in Oak Ridge, but I had sold my hogs. I was living some of the time in a mobile home near the flea market in Powell,

Tennessee, off I-75 and Emory Road, where I had a booth. Bill hadn't never done no flea marketing before, but he was retired and he wanted to help. He got real interested in it and decided to take his travel trailer to Mexico where he heard you could buy silver jewelry real cheap. He loaded up with silver and turquoise rings, bracelets, belt buckles, and stuff like that. He rented the space next to mine at the flea market, and he made good money off of it.

Me and Bill had some good times dancing, fishing, and flea marketing, but we also had our battles. Sometimes he wanted to tell me what to do, but like with a lot of my other husbands, that didn't usually turn out too good.

Bill thought I should try to control Neomi's cussing, but she was grown and I didn't think that was none of my business, and I shore didn't think it was none of his. I knowed she'd learnt that cussing from me, but I did get on to her good one time when I got pulled over for speeding in a school zone. We had just picked Jason up at his school in Oliver Springs and was still in the school zone. I didn't think I'd had time to reach a high enough speed to be over the limit. That policeman tried to say we was from out of town, but since kids from Marlowe was assigned to that school, I couldn't see what that had to do with anything. I was talking my way out of a ticket when Neomi piped up and called the cop a bald-headed son of a bitch. He not only give me a ticket, he took my license, too. I asked how I was supposed to drive home without a license, so he give me a temporary one and said I'd get mine back when I paid the forty-five dollar ticket.

Although I did blame Neomi for me having to pay that ticket, I still defended her right to cuss if she wanted to. Bill started in on that subject again one day when we was going somewhere and I was driving. I told him to hush, but he just kept on. Then he had the nerve to call me a bitch. I thought if he was a telling me to tell Neomi not to cuss, then why was he doing it? It made me mad. I took the steering wheel in my left hand and back-handed him across the mouth with my right. I didn't think I'd hit him very hard, but it broke his upper plate into two pieces.

He was not happy about that, but I told him he was gonna look a whole lot better with a brand new set of teeth.

Bill was real jealous. One time he just wouldn't let up about me hugging a biker guy who was an old friend. I was at the ironing board, pressing a skirt I was gonna wear to the jubilee that night. He leaned in toward me, just a fussing, with his thick bottle cap glasses right in my face. I whacked him with that flat iron. I didn't burn him, but I did break them ugly glasses. At the time he weren't too pleased about it, but later he told Neomi we had ironed out our differences.

Bill's three daughters lived in Charleston, South Carolina. I went there with him two or three times to see them. I insisted on picking up aluminum cans every time we seen one along the highway. It took us quite a while to get there, but I felt like the trip weren't wasted since we could sell them cans when we got back home.

When I was with Bill's family, I felt like a one-legged man at a dance. One of his daughters was married to a doctor. I think she thought her daddy was too good for me, and I could tell they wanted him back with their momma, his ex-wife, Judy. They called me a pig farmer, which was true since I had raised hogs.

The last time we visited them, when I was ready to go home Bill wanted to stay a while longer. I weren't real crazy about him staying without me, but I give in.

"Bill," I said, "I need to get back home to check on things. I know you want to stay, and I guess that's okay with me. But if you go fooling around with that ex-wife of yores it's all over but the shouting."

I went on home, but I called him one day and the maid answered the phone.

"Hey there. This here's Hazel. I need to speak to Bill."

"Hey, Miz Hazel. Mr. Bill ain't here. Him and Miz Judy's done gone skiing at the lake."

So that was that.

I told my landlord I was closing my flea market and moving out. He didn't want me to do that cause he said I had been a real good tenant.

He offered me an old building I could move into, so I cleaned my stuff out of the trailer and moved into that place.

When Bill come back home I told him I knowed what was going on with him and Judy.

"I told you not to go fooling around with that ex-wife of yores. There ain't no need for no fussing nor squabbling. You can have the mobile home if you want it. You can live in it, or you can sell it and go back to Charleston." I turned my back to walk away.

"Dammit, Hazel, you don't listen to no explanations, do you?"

I turned back around, and he hit me real hard on my cheek and left a cut. Then he hit me in the mouth, busting my lip in three different places. That made me mad, and I went for my .38.

He started to leave, but I pointed my pistol at him and said, "Stay and finish what you started, you son of a bitch."

I wanted to shoot him between the eyes, but I thought about how hard it would be on my children if I went to jail, so I lowered the gun.

"Just get on out and don't come back."

He walked toward the door, but when he reached it he turned around and looked back. He just had to say one more thing. I couldn't resist. I raised that pistol and shot him across the back of his neck. I knowed I didn't do no serious damage, but I was glad he felt it.

"Yore a crazy woman," he howled, holding on to his bloody neck as he lit out toward his car, jumped in, and took off with tires a squealing.

Later when the policeman showed up at my door with a gun in his hand, my first thought was, "Oh, no, they're gonna take my .38." I never had been put in jail, but that weren't what was worrying me most. I'd had that gun since I was a kid when Uncle Hal give it to me for protection against my daddy.

The cop had the flea market land lord with him, which made me feel a little better. I liked him a lot and knew him to be a fair sort of feller. I'd never really trusted policemen, and, to tell the truth, I feel the same way to this day. But that one was a good one. "I hear somebody got shot up here," he said, putting his pistol back in the holster. "But from the looks of yore face, I think I know why."

I was setting on the sofa and he set down next to me and said, "Boy, you are little, ain't you?

"That's why I need a gun. I have to take care of myself," I replied.

"Little girl, I'm not gonna lock you up. You have every right to protect yoreself. What I want to tell you is I'm proud of you."

He wanted me to swear out a warrant for Bill's arrest, but I said no, I weren't gonna sign no warrant. I told him this land lord here had been real good to me, and folks wouldn't want to come to a place where they knowed there'd been a shooting. I didn't want to draw no bad attention. Plus, I kind of figure me and my .38 had already settled things with Bill.

"Well, suit yoreself, Miz Lindsey," he said. "But if you change yore mind or if he bothers you again, you give us a call. And the next time you shoot him send me a picture."

There was a real nice lady that had been coming to my booth at that flea market looking for old dresses. She called them "vintage" clothes. I always kept the prettiest things back for her, and she paid me a good price for them. I didn't know she was married to the policeman that come to my place, but the next time I seen her she asked about the shooting.

"Hazel, did you shoot Bill?" she asked.

"A little bit."

"How do you shoot somebody a little bit?"

"Well, I didn't kill him." That tickled her and she laughed. I laughed, too.

I figured I'd seen the last of Bill. But before I got around to divorcing him he come to see me and asked if I'd take him back.

"Hazel, I'm sorry about how I done you. I love you, and I realize what I have lost. I'm asking you to forgive me and take me back."

"I told you when I married you I don't give no second chances."

"I know, Hazel. But I'm a changed man. And I'm sick, and I need yore help. I know taking care of me will be rough, but I don't want to spend my last days with nobody but you."

At first I didn't believe him, but finally I agreed. He had kidney cancer, and as it got worse one of the hardest times of my life was about to unfold.

I took care of Bill the best I could at home, but finally the cancer got so bad I had to check him into the Oak Ridge Hospital. At first we was back and forth. He'd get better and we'd come home. Then he'd get bad again and we'd have to go back. But the last time he stayed in the hospital for ninety-three days, and I only left him one time. He asked me to go home and cook him a piece of steak just the way he liked it. The rest of the time he wanted me right with him all the time, so I stayed by his side day and night and done everthing I could to make him comfortable.

His children never had visited him in the six years I was married to him. Now they would come see him in the hospital occasionally, but except for one daughter, they didn't seem too interested in visiting very long. Neomi come to see him all the time, making a special effort on Christmas Day to get back from visiting Dave's family and her daddy in time to spend some time with Bill. His daughters all went skiing in Vermont, even though they must of knowed it would be their daddy's last Christmas on this earth.

One daughter brought her momma to the hospital to see him. I guess she thought she still had a chance to get him back. But Bill said he didn't want to see her, so we didn't let her come in his room. Then his family got the idea he ought to be moved to a hospital in Charleston, but Bill wouldn't hear of that. He said he wanted to stay in Oak Ridge and he wanted me to take care of him. Rocky as things was when he was healthy, he knowed he could count on me to help him in his sickness.

As Bill's condition was getting worse, he got down to 80 pounds. They was feeding him through a tube to his stomach, and he was getting weaker and weaker. They wouldn't let him get no rest. Not only his doctor, but a bunch of other doctors was all the time examining him and wanting to do more tests. I couldn't see how more tests was gonna help him at this point, and I said I thought they ought to leave him be, but they didn't pay no attention to me.

The doctor finally said they had done all they could for Bill and it was just a matter of keeping him as comfortable as possible 'til the end. I knowed Bill wanted to go home, so I was preparing to check him out of the hospital and take him there. I had set up a hospital bed and arranged for Hospice to look in on him every day.

Bill's son-in-law George, who was a doctor, come to Oak Ridge and talked to the doctor that was treating Bill. I didn't know they was plotting something because I rarely left Bill's bedside.

My sister Geraldine come to the hospital in her car and was gonna take us home. She had went out to smoke a cigarette when a woman come in and said they needed to talk to me downstairs. I asked if they could wait 'til my sister got back cause Bill didn't like being left by hisself. She said no, but that she'd get somebody from the nurses' station to go set with him.

We passed a window, and, looking out, I could see an ambulance parked outside. I wondered if somebody was coming in or going out. When we got down to the office, the woman started shuffling some papers and saying stuff that didn't make no sense. I knew then something weren't right, and I went running back to Bill's room. A police woman stopped me and wouldn't let me go in. They took me to a room across the hall where they also was holding my sister. She told me she saw them rolling Bill out and they wouldn't let her come find me.

I was so upset. I started screaming and crying. I didn't know what they was doing with Bill. I had no way of knowing if he was upset. I didn't even know if he was dead or alive. I had promised I wouldn't leave him, but they had lured me out of the room and didn't even let me say good-bye. I found out later that the ambulance I seen out that window was waiting for him. They was taking him to the airport to fly him to Charleston.

Somehow Bill's family managed to get into mine and Bill's bank account and empty it out. They must of faked his name on a power of attorney, cause the doctor said there was no way he could have signed

his own name. They went to where he'd worked and changed the bene-
ficiary of his life insurance. They changed the title on his truck, and they
even had the nerve to go to our place on the lake and take everthing they
wanted. Bill had give me a painting on our first date, and they took that.

I made a bunch of phone calls to Charleston to try to talk to Bill, but
they wouldn't let me. George, his doctor son-in-law, was the only one
they'd let me talk to. He tried to say that Bill was happy with them. He
said Bill told him he'd be dead if he had stayed with me. I knowed it
weren't true cause when they took him he couldn't even talk, and I don't
think he could have got that much better. I said if he was talking, let
him tell me that hisself, but George said no.

George tried to bring up the problems Bill and me had had in our
marriage to make it look like I was an unfit – even dangerous – wife. I
said it was Bill who come asking me to take him back. I didn't go looking
for him. He could have went to Charleston when he first got sick if that
was what he wanted. I said when I promised to help him, I never went
back on my word 'til they forced me out of the picture.

I never seen Bill again. I didn't know if he was comfortable or if he
was sad. I wondered if he thought I abandoned him. When he died, his
daughter sent me a telegram. She said he was buried in a flag-draped
casket. I didn't see it cause I didn't get to go to his funeral, and, to this
day, I don't know exactly where he's buried at. All I know is they brought
him back to somewhere in Middle Tennessee. I know that, because there
was an article in the paper about his flag-draped casket in a van spotted
in a Knoxville parking lot. But by the time I learnt about that they had
already buried him.

I recorded a telephone conversation I had with George and done the
same with an argument I had with the doctor who let them take Bill
without saying nothing to me. I thought I might need to use them in a
law suit. I did take them to court, but the little lawyer I had was pretty
green, and their lawyer just walked all over him. They claimed they took
the money for sitters and other expenses. I found out they used some of

our money to pay his ex-wife to set with him. I can't imagine anything he'd of hated worse than that.

Neomi asked the doctor why he went along with George and let them take Bill out of the hospital. He told her I was a member of a motorcycle gang, which I weren't. But even if I had been, what difference would that of made?

There was one thing they wasn't able to get their hands on, though. It seems Bill was being used as a test case in a class action law suit for Oak Ridge workers who had health problems caused by exposure to radiation. Bill had worked in one of the hottest spots at the X-10 plant. That's why so many doctors – 21 in all, I found out – had examined him and done all them tests. Neomi took care of the paperwork, and I would eventually get $275,000 in the settlement. I don't think his folks ever knowed about it, but it was only give to the spouse, so they wouldn't have had no claim on it.

I didn't really need a bunch of money, so I would give each of my three kids $40,000, and each grandchild $1000, and each great-grandchild $500. I would buy each of my grandsons a truck, and, on down the road, I would use the rest to buy my own flea market.

PART III

FIREBALL AFTER THE HUSBANDS

I always worked hard, built my own houses… I'll guess when my time comes I'll have to dig my own grave.
—Hazel

CHAPTER 19:
OCTOBER SKY

After all them ordeals I had went through with my eleven husbands, I decided I didn't need to marry no more. A friend asked me didn't I want to make it an even dozen, and I said, "Naw, when it's time to quit, it's time to quit."

I thought a lot about my life – all the trials and tribulations I had endured and the really happy times, too. I got to thinking that most folks never went through near as many different adventures and alterations as me. Why, I thought, my life is like a movie – a horror movie, I joked.

So when I learnt they was coming in to make a moving picture in Oliver Springs near where I lived, I decided to go see if they might be interested in making one about my life. The movie they was getting ready for was from a book called *Rocket Boys*. It was about a teenage boy whose family was coal miners, but after he seen Sputnik pass over in 1957, all he wanted to do was shoot off rockets, not dig coal.

It was snowing on the cold January day when I went over to Oliver Springs High School where they was holding auditions. Still, the line of people waiting to see if they could be in that movie was all the way around to the end of the block. I weren't there for no try-out, but I didn't see no other place to go, so I got in line with them.

It was a long slow wait – and freezing cold too – but I didn't give up. People was all hugging their coats tight around their bodies and stamping their feet trying to keep warm, but you could tell they was excited too. This might be the only chance they'd ever get to be famous, so their hopes was high. Some of them was talking about how a famous movie star got her start just like this, waiting in line, hoping to get discovered – and she was. I didn't hear which movie star it was, and I weren't close enough to the conversation to ask.

When I finally got to the head of the line, I told the feller there I was looking for somebody to make a movie of my life cause I thought it'd be a lot more interesting than most movies I'd ever saw. He was real polite, but he told me they was registering people who wanted to be what they call "extras" in the movie. He said they didn't have no writer with them to start a new story, but would I be interested in being in this movie?

Well, I was there, and I didn't have nothing else I needed to do right then, and I thought it might be fun, so I asked, "What do I have to do?"

Hazel

They sent me over to a woman they said was the casting director, and she wrote down some stuff about me and said they'd call if they needed me. Well I guess they decided pretty quick, cause by the time I got home there was already a message waiting on my recording machine saying they wanted me to report to Morgan Field at seven o'clock in the morning. I went in like they said, and they done my makeup and give me the clothes they wanted me to wear. They said I would be the wife of a coal miner. I understood what a miner's life was like cause my son Dallas was working in the mines. Plus, I had lived around hard working folks like that all my life, so I guess they seen I'd fit right in.

That was the start of a good adventure, and I become a "movie star," or that's what I like to tell people. It weren't glamorous, and I didn't have no speaking lines nor nothing like that, but I did wail and cry when my husband died in a mine accident. Later my grandson Jason told me that's how he spotted me in the movie. He recognized my wailing before he seen me in them cat-eye glasses they'd give me to wear.

Extras waiting in line for makeup

We had to come in at four o'clock ever morning with our hair on rollers. We'd put on the movie clothes and let them fix our hair and makeup. Since I was the wife of a coal miner, there weren't nothing fancy about my look. But they had all of us females wear plastic rain bonnets to hold our hair in place like they wanted it. After they got us fixed, we mostly just waited around in a building or under a tent 'til they needed us. They called what we was doing "hurry up and wait." Days was long, too. Sometimes we was there 'til midnight and still had to be back at four in the morning. Some folk read, played cards, knitted, crocheted, or done other hobbies to pass the time. Some of us just stood around talking, wondering when they was gonna call us again to do something. They did provide our food, which was awfully good. And one of our holding places had a piano, so one of the extras, a local entertainer named Roy "Boy" Baker, who was to be my husband in the movie, would entertain us with his playing.

We might of thought it was boring at times, just sitting around, but we didn't have to work as hard as the crew. An old red brick building in Oliver Springs had been changed to the Olga Coal Company Store for the movie. Ever morning before they was gonna shoot scenes of the men walking by there on their way to work in the mines, they had to cover the paved street in front with rocks and leaves. When shooting was done for the day, they'd have to clean it all up, and then they had

Roy "Boy" Baker entertains the extras

to do the same thing again the next day. Most folks probably think they just shoot a scene one time, and that's it. But it ain't like that. Most of the time they would shoot the same scene over and over before they got it just the way they wanted it.

For one scene they had an old blue truck they needed somebody to drive. They asked who could drive a stick shift, and one of the extras named Mimi Brock said she could. They said naw, they needed a man. But they did let her ride in the passenger seat. She said that even though they only had to go a few blocks, they used up half a tank of gas doing retakes.

Part of the movie was shot nearby in Petros where they had created what looked like the entrance to the mine. When they needed us in scenes there, they'd pick us up at Morgan Field and take us there in buses.

Hazel and Roy "Boy" Baker

Sometimes we was filming next to Bushy Mountain State Penitentiary in Petros. At first we was told not to talk to the prisoners, but then they decided to use some of them in the movie. After Roy Boy, my main husband, died in the movie, they matched me up with one of them convicts. He was as nice as the other husbands, not scary at all.

Sometimes the weather was real bad, but we had to be there anyway. One time was when we was out at the field where them boys shot off rockets. We was waiting around for the big scene where the town folks come to watch the final rocket launch when it come up a bad thunderstorm. We had to run get in them antique cars that was setting around. We had to set there quite a while, but it was worth the wait when we seen a double rainbow come out. It was real pretty, and it seemed like it meant something special about the movie.

Another thing I shore won't forget about that movie was when my bloomers fell down in the middle of a scene. This time, when it was supposed to be raining, there weren't no cloud in the sky. So they rigged up some pipes and got a fire truck to shoot water up through them so it would look like rain was falling. The water was heated in them pipes, but by the time it fell on us it weren't warm no more. Me and Roy Boy was in that scene, and my clothes got so soaked my drawers fell down! Roy Boy near about died laughing. I thought it was funny, too. I weren't embarrassed at all. I just reached down and pulled them muddy britches back up and tried not to show I was holding on to them through my dress for the rest of that shoot.

At first they was calling the movie "Rocket Boys," like the book. The writer of that book was a man named Homer Hickman. He was the main boy the story was about. Jake Gyllenhaal was the actor who played him. A lot of the time Homer and his wife Linda was there when we was shooting, and they was real friendly. I had my picture took a couple of times with Homer, and one of them, along with another extra named Joyce Poe, was in the newspaper. There was also a picture of us with assistant director, Rusty Mahmood.

Joyce was a diabetic and had to have insulin twice a day. She couldn't go a long time without eating, neither. One time she said she was shaky and didn't think she could be in the next scene. So Rusty sent somebody on a three wheeler all the way back to the food tent to get her some juice and a banana. They was good to look after us like that.

Hazel and Joyce Poe

Some of the other big actors besides Jake Gyllenhaal was Chris Cooper and Laura Dern. Lots of local folks in Oliver Springs made friends with the cast and crew cause most of them was real nice. Later they changed the movie name to *October Sky*. It become a real popular movie. I heard it won some awards, but I don't know which ones they was.

The filming had started on February 23, 1998, and finished two months later on April 30. Nearly a year later, in February of 1999, we got word the picture was done and they was gonna have what they called the premiere at a movie theater in Knoxville. This would be the first time regular folks got to see the full movie. They said extras would get to go to it, but it turned out they gave out too many tickets to the stiff collars in business and government and

Barbara Hilemon and bus driver

some folks connected to the University of Tennessee, so there wasn't none left for us.

We was real disappointed about that, but one of the extras named Barbara Hilemon was a good organizer. She arranged for another premiere for the extras at the Tinseltown Movie Theater in Oak Ridge on February 19, which was Homer's birthday, another reason to celebrate. Barbara said we could watch the movie and have a party afterwards, but we'd have to pay for our movie tickets. I was okay with paying, but she asked for the money in advance. I weren't too sure I wanted to do that after being let down about the first premiere. What if this one fell through, too? How could I be sure I'd get my money back?

Barbara promised weren't nothing gonna happen this time, and she seemed like an honest lady, so I give her my money. I got all dressed up, and Neomi and Dave bought me a corsage of red roses. I guess it was kind of like a young girl getting all prettied up for the prom, which, of course, I never went to.

Roy Boy paid for a limousine to pick us up a few at a time at Morgan Field to take us to the theater. We got the red-carpet treatment, and I really did feel like a movie star that night.

Hazel arrives at the premiere of October Sky.

Hazel and Roy Boy all dolled up for the premiere.

After that, I got to work in some more movies, but they wasn't famous like *October Sky*. I don't remember what they was called. One of them was shot in Chattanooga. I liked the movie business, and I wouldn't mind being in another one if they called me. What I'd really like to do is be in a movie about my life.

Not long ago, more than fifteen years after I was in that movie, my friend Julia took me to the October Sky Festival in Oliver Springs. Barbara Hilemon was there with pictures from the making of the movie. She had sent me a book she had put together about the extras in the movie and a big picture of me getting out of that limousine, which I appreciated. It was good to connect with her again. But I was sad when she told me Roy Boy had recently passed away. And she said Joyce Poe was in a nursing home.

We took a bus tour of some of the places where the movie was shot. The tour guide was Mimi Brock, the one that rode in that blue truck for that scene that used up so much gas. I had a lot of fun, and it really brought back memories of being in that movie.

Hazel with Mimi Brock, October Sky Festival, October 18, 2014

Hazel with a display of the real Rocket Boys

Note: Most of the photos in this chapter courtesy Barbara Hilemon. They first appeared in her book, *The Making of Rocket Boys/October Sky*.

CHAPTER 20:
SWEETWATER

Over the years when me and Geraldine had drove down to Meigs County to see our momma, we'd usually leave home early in the morning so we could make it a full day. Sometimes we'd go through Kingston. Other times we'd take the faster interstate route and get off at the second Sweetwater exit that was on Highway 68. When we took this second route, there was a place between Sweetwater and Decatur where we liked to stop and eat our breakfast. It was a nice open space by the side of the road where a restaurant and gas station had stood before they burned down. Now there weren't nothing left but a concrete slab, a telephone pole, and a post with an old cast iron bell on it.

We'd pull the car over, get out, and stretch our legs, and then we'd take out the brown paper bag with the food we brung with us. Usually it was biscuits filled with homemade sausage from the hogs I raised and butchered. We'd lean against the car enjoying the sausage biscuits and the view. It was a real pretty area with hills and trees all around and a sweet little church across the road.

One day when we was stopped there a man pulled up beside us in his truck and started talking to us. He was real friendly and didn't act like he wanted to bother us none, so we carried on a little conversation with him. He asked what we was eating, and we give him a sausage biscuit. He thought it was good and said he would buy as many as we wanted to bring next time. So we got his phone number so we could call and tell him when we was coming through. I told him we could use some extra snuff money. Geraldine laughed cause she knowed didn't neither one of us dip snuff.

One morning we was resting there, and I said to Geraldine, "This would be a good place for a flea market. I think I might buy this land." Well, she just laughed at me, called me "Dummy," and said we ought to head on down the road.

Geraldine died before I got around to finding out who owned that land and set about making arrangements to rent it. I missed Geraldine a lot, so it seemed kind of right to set up at a place that had good memories of her.

After Bill died, I had got back into flea marketing, which I had stopped when he got so sick. And I was also working with an auctioneer in Anderson County. We'd haul stuff in on big old trucks, and we worked hard getting things set up beforehand. But during the auction I usually just held up items, told the value of them, took bids, and joked around with folks, so it was fun. The owner liked having me work for him, and he paid me good money. He said I done the work of three people.

We mainly had auctions in places close by like Knoxville, Cleveland, and Chattanooga, but we traveled around some, too. When we wasn't close enough to get home at night, they put me up in a motel. The owner told me I could pick out any place I wanted to stay. He was good to me like that, and I enjoyed the work. But after I signed the papers on the land near Sweetwater, renting it for three months at a time, I had to stop working auctions.

At first I'd go down on weekends and bring my little silver trailer full of merchandise to sell. I'd set up tables and sell during the day and sleep in the trailer at night. On Sunday evening I'd head back up to Oak Ridge. But when my flea market business in Sweetwater got going real good, I spent more time there.

I was getting a lot of items, a truck load at a time, from the Supply House in Marlowe. They got stuff from the county dump in Oak Ridge and cleaned it up. Neomi said all the men there, especially the one they called Tater Bug, was in love with me and so they saved the best things that come through for me. She also liked to tease me about something that happened when I had a load of salvaged items on my truck, a lot of it metal, and I made a wrong turn.

I was suppose to be heading from Oak Ridge down Highway 95 toward Sweetwater with my load, but somehow I turned into the X-10 plant entrance. I notice the guard waving at me, and I waved right back and kept going. I crossed a pretty little bridge and was trying to turn around when the guard, who had jumped in his car and come after me, yelled out his window asking me what the hell I thought I was doing.

I seen I was right next to where Neomi worked, and I hoped she wouldn't see me. But somebody told her to come look out the window. He said some woman with a load of junk on her truck had just crashed through the guard gate. Neomi looked out and weren't surprised to see it was me. By the time she got out there I had already explained my mistake to that guard, and he was gonna let me go. Neomi said, "Momma, they could have took you for a terrorist and shot you, coming inside a restricted area with a load of metal like that. Just think of the damage you could of done if you had a bomb in that truck."

Things was going good in Sweetwater. A man named Matthew who worked at the Watts Bar Dam in Ten Mile up the road a piece took to stopping by on a regular basis. He flirted with me and flattered me, and the next thing I knowed, we was a dating. And before long I moved in with him. He wanted to marry me, but I weren't interested in that.

Hazel and Matthew

Matthew said he wanted to invest in my business, so he took out a mortgage on his house and bought the land. He become my partner, and I started making payments to him for my share.

Meanwhile, me and Jason made a deal to tear down an old dormitory in Oak Ridge like the one I had lived in when I first come up there before I married Amos. They said they would give us the wood in exchange for tearing it down. Me and Jason worked real good together. He would pull off the boards and I'd take the nails out real careful not to bend them so we could use them again. We took that wood to Sweetwater to put up my first permanent building there.

I bought a used full-size trailer, and me and Jason gutted the insides and remodeled it for me a nice place to live in. I really needed to be there twenty-four seven, otherwise folks would steal me blind.

Over the next ten years I brought seven trailers and we built several wooden buildings from dormitories and other buildings we tore down. We moved some in from other places, too, including a corn crib that I had built years ago in Decatur. Jason's friend Casey helped some with the building, and my brother Lester helped with sheet metal work and the stove pipe installation for my wood-burning cook stove, but me and Jason did most of the work. I was getting up in years by this time, but I hadn't slowed down none.

Things wasn't working out too good between me and Matthew. I never knowed a man who was willing to work as hard as me, and he weren't no exception. So when that money from the settlement related to Bill's illness come from Oak Ridge, I told him I wanted to buy him out. He said I could do that, but the land was worth a lot more now since all them improvements had been made, so I would have to pay more than what he had put into it. I didn't think that was quite fair since me and Jason had did all the work to make them improvements, not him. But that's the only way he would sell it, so I paid him what he said, and I swore then and there I weren't never going into no more partnerships.

I liked the freedom I had now to do things like I wanted to. I was in my seventies, and it was hard work, but not near as hard as most other times of my life. I didn't have to keep no regular schedule or deal with lots of employees like when I run my restaurant. It was messy, but so was upholstering and slopping hogs. And for a kid who didn't have nothing, it was a thrill to look around me and see all them buildings stuffed with things I could sell.

Aerial view of Hazel's salvage/junkyard/flea market near Sweetwater.

There was some problems, though. A county official said I weren't supposed to have so many buildings on that small a space. But I joked with him that I didn't know how it happened, but them first buildings just kept having babies. Finally he quit pestering me about it.

The next door neighbors wasn't too pleased, neither, to see all that salvaged merchandise – they called it junk – accumulating, so I put up a privacy fence between me and them. And the church people across the road had to put in their two cents worth about it, too. They said it was an eyesore and wanted to tell me what I could and couldn't do with my own property that I had bought and paid for myself. That made me mad, so I just junked it up even worse. I told them if I come to church over there, they probably wouldn't like how I was dressed in blue jeans. And they had a right to feel that way cause it was their property. But they didn't have no right to come to mine and tell me what I had to do.

Later they started acting nice about it, so I neatened it up some and moved things further back from the road. But I did give them a warning. When my brother Lester and some of our friends started bringing their guitars so we could pick and sing our hearts out in that first building Jason and me built, I told them that it weren't all gonna be gospel.

Hazel and friends

I made friends with a lot of the people who stopped by to buy or sell things, and I had me a pretty good business going. Some of the men acted like they was interested in buying something, but they wasn't gonna get what they was really there for. One wannabe asked me, "Hazel, when are you gonna let me take you to bed?"

I said, "When I get too feeble to get there by myself."

From what I'd been told, I had outlived all my eleven husbands, and I didn't intend to have no more. But I usually had a boyfriend or two hanging around. Not long ago one asked me to marry him, and I said, "You can put a ring on my finger, but I ain't gonna sign no papers."

It turned out that feller weren't no good. He hadn't gotten around to putting no ring on my finger, and I was glad I hadn't signed no papers with him. That way there wasn't no complications when I sent him on his way.

I do like having a bed feller ever now and then. A woman asked me, "Hazel, when did you stop having sex?"

I told her, "I'm eighty-three years old, and I ain't there yet."

Hazel and Pat, a friend she calls Josephine, July, 2014. Photo by David Adams.

Hazel and long-time neighbor Jace

I wouldn't leave my place no more than was necessary, so when I did go somewhere I was always in a hurry to get home. One day I got pulled over by a Monroe County policeman, who said I was speeding. He asked to see my driver's license and registration. When he seen my name on the license, he asked me was I the woman who owned that flea market out on sixty-eight. I said I was. He said, "My daddy would have a fit if I arrested you!"

Since I was kind of nervous, I'd give him my gun permit instead of registration papers. When he looked at it, he said, "Oh, my God. You got a loaded gun, too." But since the gun was legal and he didn't want to

Hazel (beyond white truck) making a deal to buy some merchandise.

upset his daddy, I got off with just a warning that time.

One day I got a surprise visit from somebody I hadn't saw in seventeen or eighteen years. He showed up wearing cowboy boots and hat and a big old silver belt buckle. Unlike me, he had got a whole lot older, so I didn't recognize him 'til he told me who he was. His name was Charlie Muncie, and I used to dance with him up at Ciderville.

He said he had been dancing all night and his legs was a hurting, but he come looking for his favorite dance partner. He said he seen Dallas' wife Clara and she told him where he could find me. He asked me to go dancing with him that night. I said I would if he was paying. Some men think if they get a hold of an old woman like me she'll be happy to pay for everthing. But not me. I don't support no man. He agreed to pay, and we went and had us a good old time at the Pickin' Parlor on Highway 11 in Athens.

These last fifteen years running my salvage business has been the most peaceful of my life. I'm doing what I like and I ain't got nobody trying to boss me around. But there has been some sadness, too. Both of my older sisters has died now, and I miss them.

* * *

A few years ago I met somebody who was gonna help me make a dream come true. But, of course, we didn't know that at the time. Her name was Julia, and she come to my place looking to see if I had an old claw-foot bathtub she could buy. We hit it off right away. We both liked reusing old stuff – and I had a lot of that – stead of buying new things all the time.

Julia come by my place from time to time, and she liked hearing me tell about my life growing up in Meigs County and the tales of all them husbands. When I found out she was a writer, I got real excited. I asked her if she'd write my life story. She said she'd think about it. She had some other project she needed to finish first.

One day she come by with some papers where she had wrote down some of my stories. She said I should show them to Neomi and Dallas and see if they was okay with her writing my book and telling my stories like they really happened. I had told her I didn't want nothing that weren't true in it. I said I'd take them pages next time I went up to Oak Ridge.

But it were a while before I could get back to thinking about the book. My son Dallas was real sick, and he died of cancer on Jan. 25, 2013. He had left working in the mines and had gone into business with Neomi's husband, Dave. They was co-owners of Davenport Tree and Landscaping Company. He was always good with his hands. His obituary in the newspaper said, "If it could be made, Dallas Ricker could fix it," which was true. It also said how he loved riding Harley Davidson motorcycles and going fishing at the Outer Banks of North Carolina. I knowed he got that love of fishing from my momma, but I don't know where he got the love of motorcycle riding from. It shore weren't from me or Mommy.

I was real proud of Dallas, and it made me so sad to lose another child. Although he was sixty-four years old, he was still one of my babies. I

Dallas and Claire with Taynia, Troy, and Amanda

weren't myself for some time after he died. And with Neomi being my only child left, and her health not too good, I begin to thinking that maybe I ought to sell my place at Sweetwater and move back to my house near Oak Ridge so I could have more time with her and Dave and Jason. Weren't none of us getting no younger. Jason had a daughter of his own, now. Her name was Kaitlyn, and it wouldn't be long before she would be a mother herself.

So I was back and forth a lot between my two places for the next couple of years while me and Julia worked on our book. It made me feel real good to look back and see what I had accomplished. And I think my momma would have been proud of me. I don't steal nor lie, like she said. I still don't drink no whiskey, and I don't date no married men. I ain't quit cussing yet, but most of the time when I call somebody a son of a bitch, he ain't no stranger.

Epilogue

A fireball moves in one direction – forward. And that describes Hazel perfectly. She was always looking ahead to possible opportunities. She never let the past drag her down for long. Many people who have had harsh beginnings and lost precious children and a most beloved husband spend many years in therapy. Some inner quality allowed her to grieve and moved on. While writing this book, the times she teared up were in describing the losses of Polly Jean and James Trueblood. Of the later, she said, "I did know how to love a man."

Though, at 84, her body and mind are slowing down somewhat, she is still in excellent health. She has all her teeth, her hearing is good, she wears glasses only for reading, and her hair has more brown stands than gray. She rarely takes medicine, although her doctor did prescribe blood thinners and iron tablets. She says medicine is for when you feel bad, and since she usually feels fine, she doesn't bother to take them.

And in spirit she remains a fireball. She usually has a boyfriend or two and a few "wannabees" hanging around. Not long ago she had a bad sore on her leg that took a long time to heal. Her daughter took her to her dermatologist for treatment. He got such a kick out of Hazel that he told his receptionist to save some extra time in his schedule whenever she had an appointment so he'd have time to talk to her. During the examination, he noticed a dark spot on her face that he thought might be troublesome. He said he'd like to do a biopsy. Hazel told him he could, but she said he should be careful and not mess up her face because she might want to get married again. "And you know," she said, "men are only interested in looking at two places, and one of them is the face."

In recent months Hazel has moved back and forth between her home and business in Sweetwater and one she built in the Marlow community near Oak Ridge. Her daughter Naomi (the name she now goes by) lives in the first house she built there, the one where she lived with Amos and raised, or finished raising, three of her natural children and four step children. Her grandson Jason lives between his mother's and Hazel's houses. Every evening he comes to see her or calls to say good night. She enjoys being near Naomi, Dave, and Jason, yet she likes her independence and misses the friends in Sweetwater. When she is there, a stream of regular visitors are constantly dropping by, bringing a pizza, a hamburger, or other edibles. She has little need to cook, but keeps a good supply of bologna, white bread, and Coca Colas on hand.

Hazel still enjoys going to country jubilees. Sometimes she returns to Ciderville Music Barn on a Saturday night, and can frequently be spotted on a Friday night buck dancing at the McMinn County Senior Center in Athens. Her voice is still strong, and if you drop by to see her, with a little encouragement, she'll sing one of her original songs for you.

Hazel and I hope you have enjoyed reading her story as much as have we enjoyed telling it. Hazel is pleased with the book, but still talks about our movie. She is sure it's going to be a good one.

Julia Walker

APPENDIX

Some things that has changed and some things that ain't changed:

- A road now runs all the way through our holler in Meigs County where I growed up. A lot of the shacks I built are still standing, though most of them is falling in or growed over with weeds and vines.

- The Oak Terrace restaurant in Oak Ridge is now a law office.

- Neomi and Dave still live in the house I built when I was married to Amos. They have added more rooms to it. About half the acres I bought in that Marlow community now belongs to somebody else. Dallas and Butch sold their land the day I deeded it to them. Although the rest of the land is in Neomi's name, I still have a house we consider mine.

- The building that was Hazel's Grill burned down twenty-five years ago except for the concrete blocks in the back. They rebuilt it, and now the Buffalo Grill is in that space.

- The building where I had Hazel's Upholstery was tore down three years ago, and now there's a parking lot for the Roane Community College where it had stood.

- I still go to Ciderville on a Saturday night ever now and then. Here's David West introducing me and telling folks what fun we used to have back in the Roaring Eighties.

- Amos got married again to a woman named Lillian. Later Buddy married Lillian's daughter Anna, and they had a little girl they named Paula. So Amos and Lillian was Paula's double grandparents. I thought that was kind of unusual.

- Here's my stepdaughter Patsy and her seven kids.

- All of my husbands are dead. Neomi is the only one of my natural children that's still living. My step children are all gone, as well, except for Andra Mae, who lives in Louisiana. All of my younger brothers and sisters, except for Geraldine, is still alive.

- I live by myself, and I ain't scared. But I wouldn't open my door at night without my Annie Oakley.

- My friend Marty, who calls me "dahling," did some looking and found out where my last husband, Bill Lindsey, is buried at. It's not too far from where I live, but I ain't been to see it yet.

- Except for Jason, I don't see my grandchildren very much. I have a great, great grandson, Rylan Jason Watson. He's Jason's grandson. I taught him to stick out his tongue.

Jason and Hazel

Hazel and Rylan

- I still love fishing. Here I am at a lake in Kingston, Tennessee.

ACKNOWLEDGEMENTS

Hazel and I wish to express our gratitude to all who assisted and encouraged us in putting her life's story into print. First, we'd like to thank those who shared their memories.

We could not have done this book without the support of Naomi (Neomi) Gibbs Davenport. Her father was the second of Hazel's husbands, so she had knowledge of all those that followed and was instrumental in jogging her mother's memory. When I first asked Hazel the names of her husbands, she replied, "Some of them wasn't worth remembering, but Neomi has them all wrote down somewhere." Naomi was also helpful in identifying photographs and putting events into the proper time slot.

Naomi's son, Jason Watson, shared his memories on a delightful Sunday afternoon drive around the Oak Ridge area. He pointed out houses, restaurants, cemeteries, music halls, and other places that were significant to Hazel during the years she lived there.

Details were provided for the October Sky chapter by Barbara Hilemon, who also allowed generous use of photographs from her book *The Making of Rocket Boys/October Sky*. Mimi Brock filled in additional details while reminiscing with Hazel on an October Sky Festival tour of Oliver Springs.

David West, owner of the Ciderville Music Barn, spent an afternoon recalling with Hazel tales of the "Roaring Eighties." Others, appreciated but too numerous to mention, dropped little tidbits here and there that helped us put it all together.

Paulette Jones of the Meigs County Historical Society was especially encouraging and helpful, as were Betty Carolyn Ward, Cathy Ricker, and others in Decatur who provided background information. Librarians at both the Meigs County and Oak Ridge public libraries and the folks at the Oak Ridge Tourism Association were most generous with their assistance.

The other group we wish to acknowledge are those who helped to make a book from Hazel's stories. I can't say enough about my brother, Norman McMillan. Author (*Distant Son* and other works) and a retired college English professor, he edited and critiqued numerous drafts, helping me keep true to Hazel's voice. His wife, Joan, using her excellent secretarial skills and her knowledge of law, also read, made suggestions, and helped with editing.

My other brothers and sisters, my three daughters, and my husband, Allen, who passed away as I was nearing completion of the book, were all encouraging, as were my five grandchildren and numerous friends.

Fellow writers of the Etowah Writer's Guild read, critiqued, and supported the writing at every stage. I am especially indebted to the late Grant Fetters, a non-southerner, who admitted his confusion with my earliest attempts to write Hazel's speech phonetically. I am especially appreciative of the support of Fran Dorwood (*Damn Greed* and other works) who led me to that group. I must also mention Debi Gregg, who believed so strongly in the book that she pushed me to explore my options with publishers when I was reluctant.

Scott Danforth of the University of Tennessee Press saw value in publishing Hazel's memoir early on. Although we decided that her story would not be best served by making it the academic work Dan would have liked to see, nevertheless, his early enthusiasm was most encouraging.

Thanks are also in order to the *Daily Post Athenian* which published the introduction and some brief excerpts from the book and allowed me to include contact information for those wanting to reserve a signed copy.

Diana Cruze, author of *A Life in the Day of a Lady Salesman*, was helpful and encouraging when we made the decision to self-publish. She put me in touch with Steve Passiouras at bookow.com who was prompt and efficient in designing the interior of the book.

Lisa Bell (lisabellfineart.com) took my basic ideas and used her artistic skill to turn them into an attractive cover.

Made in the USA
Charleston, SC
30 September 2015